Setting Up The Perfect Hunting Bow

Bill Winke

Petersen's Bowhunting Magazine
6385 Flank Drive, Suite 800
Harrisburg, PA 17112
www.bowhuntingmag.com

299. 20285
WIN

Setting Up The Perfect Hunting Bow

Editor: Christian Berg
Associate Editor: Daniel Beraldo
Copy Editors: Tony Peterson, Carolyn Olson
Art Director: Nicole Mahany
Cover Design: Jim Pfaff
Cover Image: Kevin Howard
Publisher: Petersen's Bowhunting

Most of the photographs in the chapters to follow were taken by the author, Bill Winke. The author also wishes to thank Petersen's Bowhunting's Daniel Beraldo and Tony Peterson, who also contributed photographs for this book.

First Edition
Second Printing, October 2011
Library of Congress Cataloging-in-Publication Data
ISBN (10) = 1-934622-98-2
ISBN (13) = 978-1-934622-98-8

Contents

Introduction

This book has a simple goal: to help you set up a hunting bow that is extremely accurate, idiot-proof and reliable in the field. Along the way, I will teach you how a bow works and how to get the best performance out of it through careful selection of accessories.

All the cables, strings and cams may seem intimidating on the surface, but in reality a compound bow is a very simple machine. It is a set of levers and a few strings to pivot those levers. That is all. A basic understanding of how that machine works is a great starting point.

Once you understand the basics, I'll move on to bring you more of the hands-on portion of the book I'm sure you will find most interesting. However, you can't build a house without a foundation, so you shouldn't try to build your understanding of bow mechanics and maintenance without a solid grasp of the fundamentals. The first couple of chapters are a slow start, but please be patient; things get moving from there, and with your newly acquired knowledge, you will find everything that follows makes a lot more sense.

You're sitting at the starting line of an off-road race. You're going to be out there for a while, and more than likely you will experience a few difficulties along the way: a broken belt, a bent tie-rod — it's all part of the fun. You won't be near any gas stations, repair shops or mechanics. Now, suppose you're sitting there without the foggiest clue how your vehicle works nor how to fix common problems — and you didn't bring any tools. I would say your hopes of finishing that race are kind of grim. You had better hope for a lot of luck because a tough race is going to take a toll.

In many ways, that is the way many bowhunters face each season. You are out there on your own much of the time, far from the bow shop, or facing problems at times when the shop is not open Or just as bad, you don't even realize when you are having problems that could have been easily fixed had you caught them early enough.

You are hoping that everything works the way it is supposed to. Bows are like cars and the off-road race is like a tough season of bowhunting. Just as you'd never go into the race without at least a basic understanding of how the car works and a few tools to fix it, you should apply that same logic to the upcoming hunting season.

Getting the most out of your bow — and thus your season–requires at least some involvement, interest and understanding. You can get by with a cobbled together bow rig — anything that lobs an arrow — just as you can possibly complete the off-road race with a Chevy Blazer you bought at Smilin' Sam's used car lot. But why would you intentionally limit your chances when the skills and knowledge to raise the bar are not overly taxing? Not only that, but these skills are fun to acquire and fun to use.

I am going to keep the language simple and focus on making this book as practical as possible. It is my goal that when you are done reading it you will say, "Hmm, I can do this." Chapter by chapter, I intend to help you build your understanding. Then over the next few months, you will turn your bow into a fine-tuned, lethal hunting machine. Now let's dig in. There is a lot of ground to cover and a lot of fun to be had along the way.

Bill Winke
February 2009

Chapter 1

HOW A BOW WORKS

If you're serious about being a more effective bowhunter, it's time to build a foundation — an understanding of how a bow works. But, before you start pulling axles and unfastening strings, slow down a little and let's get this machine figured out. That's where this journey will start.

HOW ENERGY IS STORED

Any time you flex a spring you cause it to store energy. If you take a coil spring and compress it, you have added energy in it. If you release the compression, the spring will straighten back out and give up the energy. It's the same with the limbs on a bow. They are simply springs (cantilever springs). With a compound bow, the limb tips aren't flexed backward toward the shooter by the string like they are with a traditional recurve that has no cams. Instead, the string and harnesses pull the limb tips toward each other. Here's how it works.

UNDERSTANDING THE ECCENTRIC SYSTEM

The basic eccentric system on a compound is made up of a string, one or two eccentrics (or cams) and one or two harnesses or cables (a modern single cam uses only one cam and a power cable). With a traditional two-cam bow, one end of the harness attaches to a peg on the

Your bow begins to store energy as soon as you begin to draw the string.

cam. The other end is attached to the axle on the opposite limb tip. When you draw the string, you pull the eccentrics around and that wraps the harnesses up and pulls the limb tips toward each other. Two-cam bows have two harnesses that work together to flex the limbs.

Single-cam bows, on the other hand, have only one harness that is used to pull the limb tips toward each other. When you draw the string, the cam turns and does two things at once. It lets the string out on the front and back while at the same time wrapping up the power cable to flex the limbs. The result is the same, the limb tips bend toward each other and the bow stores energy.

The shape of the cam determines how the draw feels and also determines how much energy the bow stores. Bow engineers tweak the shape to make cams perform the way they want them to. They can make bows faster by causing the draw force to come up quickly as soon as you start pulling on the string where the curve remains high before dropping off into the letoff valley. That bow will store a lot of energy and has the potential to be faster than a bow that comes up to maximum draw weight more smoothly and slowly.

HOW LETOFF OCCURS

An eccentric cam is just a convenient way to package two levers — a teeter-totter, if you will. One arm of the teeter-totter extends from the harness to the axle and the other extends beyond that from the axle out to the string. In a sense, the teeter-totter has two children unequal in weight moving in toward the pivot and back out toward the end to gain an advantage on each other to make it pivot. You can see this for yourself by watching the eccentrics while pulling back on the string. At first, the string will be close to the axle and then will move away. The harness will start away from the axle and then come in close.

You get "letoff" when the harness is right next to the axle. The string now has maximum leverage. The small child is then sitting at the end of the teeter-totter while balancing a much larger child sitting right next to the pivot point. Because of this mechanical advantage, you don't need to pull very hard to keep the stiff limbs flexed at full draw and storing lots of energy.

WHY BOWS FEEL DIFFERENT AT FULL DRAW

Some bows have a hard back wall in the letoff valley while others are softer. The feel of the back wall is related to the shape of the harness track in the area of letoff. This, again, is the area the harness contacts when it comes closest to the axle at the end of the draw. If the track is flat and long here, the cam can't rotate any farther — the harness pretty much locks it from turning farther. The back wall will be very solid. If the track is rounded in this area, you can easily pull the cam a bit farther. The back wall will be soft and mushy.

Bow designers also produce a solid back wall by using draw stops. These small pegs or modules attach to the cam and either contact the limb at full draw to stop the draw or they come around and contact the harness to stop the cam rotation. Either way, these draw stops represent a mechanical method of stopping the draw cold.

Regardless of how the solid wall is created, you definitely want a bow that has this feature. A solid wall produces a consistent draw length. When aiming at full draw you need something concrete and unchanging you can pull against.

WHY SOME BOWS ARE FASTER

Arrow speed is measured using a standard method so we can get an apples-to-apples comparison. The most popular current standard is what is referred to as IBO speed. This is the recorded speed when shooting a 350-grain arrow from a 70-pound bow with a 30-inch draw length through a certified chronograph. IBO speed is not the actual speed you can expect the bow to shoot unless you have those exact specifications, but it does permit us a standard for comparison. A fast bow is one that has an IBO speed over 320 fps (feet per second). Typically, most hunting models have IBO speeds over 300 fps.

Arrow speed depends upon three factors: the design of the cam, the distance from the string to the back of the grip with the bow undrawn (this is called brace height) and the bow's efficiency.

Cam shape: As I mentioned earlier, designers can set up the lever arms in the cams any way they want. They can design the cam so that it causes the bow to store a lot of energy. Or, they can design the levers so the draw is softer and smoother and more comfortable.

High-energy bows always feel like they draw harder than bows that store less energy, even though the peak draw weights are the same on both. The more

Cam design affects many characteristics of the draw cycle. Manufacturers can design the cam so it stores more energy or so it has a softer and smoother draw cycle. The shape of the cam's harness track also affects how the bow feels at full draw. Pictured is a cam with a flat track. This design promotes a solid back wall at full draw.

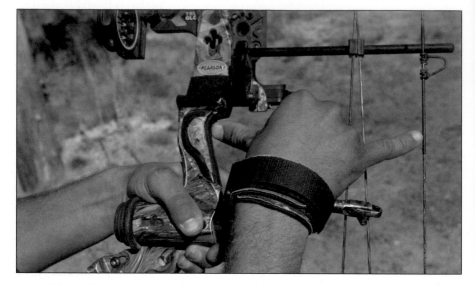

Brace height is the distance from the deepest part of the back of the grip to the string.

energy stored, the harder the bow feels and the faster it shoots, all other things being equal.

Brace height: The shorter the brace height (again, the distance from the back of the grip to the string) the greater the potential for speed. When the bow has a short brace height, you must draw the string farther to reach the same draw length. Potential energy (the fancy name for stored energy) is defined as force times distance; so anytime you increase the distance of the pull you increase the energy the bow stores.

Efficiency: Efficiency is the ability of the bow to give back the energy you put into it. It is actually a comparison of energy: divide the amount of kinetic energy in the arrow as it leaves the bow by the amount of stored energy in the limbs at full draw. This ratio will always be less than one. The lost energy is due to friction in the eccentrics, cable guard slide/harness system and any kinetic energy contained in the limbs, string and harnesses after the arrow is gone. This leftover energy, by the way, creates vibration that causes bow noise.

The most efficient bows on the market today have efficiency ratings in the range of 80 to 85 percent. The more efficient the bow, the faster it will be. Obviously, a bow with high efficiency is good. Efficiency drops off as you increase draw weight or decrease arrow weight. That's why a lighter arrow doesn't penetrate quite as well as a heavier arrow — the light arrow has soaked up less of the bow's energy on release and there is more energy left behind for the bow to dissipate through vibration. That creates noise. The lighter arrow produces a noisier shot.

YOUR ARROW'S KINETIC ENERGY

To determine your arrow's kinetic energy, you need to know two things: the arrow's weight in grains and the arrow's speed in feet per second. Weight is most accurately attained with a grain scale, while a chronograph is commonly used to accurately measure speed. Unfortunately, not every bowhunter has access to these instruments, and a trip to the local archery shop might be out of the question. Here are some tips for calculating weight and speed without expensive equipment.

Arrow weight without a grain scale: You can get very close to your finished arrow weight using the following estimates for each component and referring to your arrow company's literature or their website to get the shaft weight:

Five-inch vanes (per 3): 30 grains	**Two-inch vanes (per 3):** 15 to 25 grains
Four-inch vanes (per 3): 25 grains	**Nock system:** 20 to 30 grains*
Five-inch feathers (per 3): 20 grains	**Inserts for aluminum arrows:** 30 to 50 grains*
Four-inch feathers (per 3): 15 grains	**Inserts for carbon arrows:** 15 to 25 grains*

* Weight depends on shaft style. Generally, you can fine-tune this information by looking online at the arrow manufacturer's website.

Arrow speed without a chronograph: You can approximate your arrow speed using the following table. First, shoot your bow at a target from 20 yards using your 20-yard pin. Mark the center of your group. Next, shoot from 40 yards, still using your 20-yard pin and aiming at the same point on the target as before. Mark the center of this group, and measure the distance between the two centers. Refer to the table for your arrow speed.

Spread between 20 & 40 yard groups (inches)	Approximate Arrow Speed (fps)
19.3	190
15.8	210
13.2	230
11.1	250
9.5	270
8.3	290
7.2	310
6.4	330

Doing the calculations: Use the following formula to calculate your arrow's kinetic energy. Use finished arrow weight expressed in grains and arrow speed in feet per second.

KE (ft-lb) = arrow weight (grains) divided by 450,240 X arrow speed (fps) squared. **KE = M/450,240 X Velocity**

Recommended standards: There is no hard and fast minimum for kinetic energy when shooting at game. Some experts feel the minimum should be 45 foot pounds of arrow energy for whitetail deer and 55 foot pounds for elk and caribou. I have personally seen deer harvested cleanly with arrows having as little as 30 foot pounds of kinetic energy. Most states have minimum draw weight and minimum arrow weight laws, but few have minimum kinetic energy laws.

LOOKING AHEAD

In the next chapter, I will get into the subject of how a bow's design either makes it more accurate or less accurate. That will help you make some good decisions when buying and setting up the most accurate bow possible. However, now I want to get back to the practical side of this book. After all, it is not a study manual for high school physics, but a book about setting up the perfect hunting bow. I want you to be shooting an arrow so accurately that you can light a match at 10 yards.

Remember, this is simpler than it may appear on the surface. Bear with me through the rough spots; it all serves a purpose of making you a better-educated, more successful bowhunter. A compound bow is nothing more than a couple of fancy teeter-totters tied together with cables. It is no big deal. We're going to make those teeter-totters work as well as we possibly can.

To work on your bow you will need some basic tools and some modest mechanical skills. Thankfully, this isn't as hard as programming your VCR (or in an attempt to stay current, I'll change that to DVR). I will get into the subject of tools in Chapter 3 and how to use them in Chapter 4.

Sit back and get comfortable, this is going to be a fun journey. Next, I'm going to guide you through the subject of accuracy, where it comes from and how to make sure you have it.

Chapter 2

UNDERSTANDING ACCURACY

I f we always made perfect shots, we wouldn't need a forgiving bow. The term "forgiving" assumes there is some kind of flaw in our shooting that actually needs forgiveness. Let's look at a typical release scenario to see where the problems lie. Once we find them we can see how a bow's design can help overcome them.

Most bowhunters have at least a couple shooting flaws. We all have them to varying degrees. Most commonly, they are target panic and creeping.

Target panic is the biggest problem most archery hunters fight, whether or not they are even aware of it. By triggering the release with a mental "Now!" command, the left side of the body knows what the right side is about to do and reacts. At the same time the archer punches the trigger to try to time the pin's movement across the intended target, he snaps his hand shut on the grip or flips the bow with his wrist to make up for a pin that is not quite on the target. It is all very much unintended and even subconscious in most cases, but it is still a problem that hurts accuracy.

Because the left hand is snapping shut on the grip at the same time the release jaws are opening, the arrow is still on the string when the bow begins to move. The longer the arrow is attached to the string, the more the bow can influence it, ruining accuracy and consistency.

Creeping is another bad habit that will make you less accurate. It is the tendency to shorten your draw while aiming — to collapse a little. It is hard to tell when you are doing it, but it is easy for someone else to see just by watching your arrow slide forward across the rest. Creeping is caused by a failure on the archer's part to continue pulling the string against the back wall using his back muscles.

With these two common shooting faults in mind, I'll look at bow design with an eye toward finding ways to help you keep your arrows in the kill zone.

BRACE HEIGHT

As mentioned in the last chapter, brace height is the distance from the back of the grip to the string when the bow is at rest. I've already mentioned that a low brace height produces extra energy storage and increases arrow speed, but there is also a negative effect. Bows with short brace heights tend to be less forgiving. The arrow stays on the string for a longer distance (a longer time) as it moves forward, offering more time for a rough release to spoil the shot.

Similarly, the shape of the riser can add to forgiveness. Here's what I mean. As the distance from the back of the grip to the string increases, the riser design itself becomes more stable and resistant to turning.

As always, there is a tradeoff. My goal every time I choose a hunting bow is to find one that strikes the proper balance between speed and forgiveness. Consequently, I prefer bows with brace heights in the 7- to 7.5-inch range. It is a good range for most other bowhunters, as well.

Good archers who trigger the release by surprise don't benefit as much from a high brace height as an average archer who commands the trigger, but they too have opportunities to torque the bow. Again, the sooner the arrow is off the string, the less affect even these minor disruptions will have.

The most forgiving bow is not always the most accurate when hunting. Arrow speed plays a bigger factor in hunting accuracy than it does in target accuracy.

However, since accuracy is also dependent on speed (when the distance isn't known) the expert archer can benefit from the speed offered by a lower brace height while still maintaining pinpoint target range accuracy.

MASS WEIGHT

A forgiving bow should have a little heft to it. You'll see top target and 3-D shooters adding weight to their bows near the limb pockets–as far from the grip as possible. Pushing weight away from the grip will do the most good to oppose herky-jerky movements of the bow. It is tougher to turn and move a heavy bow quickly. This makes the bow a little more stable while aiming and shooting. You simply can't whip it around like a twig.

When it comes to shooting a hunting bow accurately, the best I know is Randy Ulmer. He recently had this to say: "Being primarily a western hunter, I'm willing to trade a little forgiveness for reduced bow weight. Every season I go on extended hunts. I have gotten my bow down to five pounds, which proves to be a definite advantage on stalks that take hours. But, if I only hunted from treestands I'd carry a bow weighing 6 to 7 pounds. And I'd use a 10- to 12-inch stabilizer to further improve forgiveness."

I just went out and weighed my current hunting bow and it comes in right at 6.5 pounds without the quiver attached. It is over 7 pounds with the quiver attached. I have never seen a situation where the bow seemed too

The bow's weight also affects its stability and accuracy.

heavy to me. In my opinion, too much is made of super lightweight bows that are on the market right now. Are we getting so lazy we can't carry an extra pound or two the half mile to our treestand? Granted, on a daylong hunt in the mountains, a couple of extra pounds may seem more significant, but even then, it is barely noticeable in my opinion.

My advice is this: don't get too carried away trying to buy the lightest bow on the market. If the bow you choose is a little heavy, that will actually work to your advantage, creating more stability.

LENGTH

A forgiving bow should be long. For the same reasons that moving weight away from the grip increases a bow's inertia, making the bow longer also increases inertia and stability. This is where the modern subcompact bow falls short of being highly forgiving. When I was starting out, a long bow was 43 inches long. Now, a long bow is 36 or 37 inches long. An inch or two either way won't make a noticeable difference, so if you are wringing your hands trying to decide between a 33-inch bow and a 36-inch bow, you can rest easier. It won't make much difference.

However, if you are trying to decide between a 33-inch bow and a 41-inch bow, that is another matter. In that case, the longer bow will be noticeably more stable and accurate.

Of the three aspects of bow design that have the most affect on forgiveness, brace height is most important. In other words, you can get by with a short bow as long as the brace height is reasonable (over 7 inches, preferably over 7.5 inches),

A cam is simply a system of levers – like a teeter-totter.

but a longer and heavier bow with the same brace height has the potential to be slightly more accurate.

CAM DESIGN

Cam design affects a bow's accuracy. Highly aggressive cams that come up to peak weight quickly and then drop sharply off into the letoff valley accelerate an arrow more violently than softer cams and round wheel bows. When an arrow receives a huge amount of energy over a short amount of time, any inconsistency in the arrow (such as a slightly bent nock) or a rough release will show up more noticeably in the accuracy of the arrow.

Another aspect of cam design that has even more affect on the forgiveness and accuracy of your bow is the solidness of the back wall at full draw. I touched on this a little bit in the last chapter, but I will get into this subject in a little more detail here.

If you change your draw length by just one half-inch from one shot to the next, you may shoot as much as three inches high or low at 20 yards and much more at longer distances. This is because some bows are more sensitive than others to inconsistent draw length. It is very hard, short of testing every bow with a shooting machine, to determine if a certain bow is forgiving or unforgiving. So, rather than try to sort that out, simply look for bows with solid back walls at full draw. That way, you are able to better control the consistency of your draw. The bow itself may be unforgiving of changes in draw length, but if you never change your draw length, who cares.

By pulling solidly into the back wall on every shot, you have a much better chance of being consistent. It is not good if you sight the bow in one way and then shoot at game another way. A solid back wall will help you be more consistent and that makes the bow more accurate.

WHY NOT JUST HUNT WITH A TARGET BOW?

Of course, the most forgiving bow you can buy is the long-standing "target" bow most of the top "paper punchers" shoot. That's no coincidence. When tournaments are won and lost by a hair's breadth, the top shooters use the absolute most accurate equipment they can find. So, why not just hunt with a target bow?

It's a good question, and I know of some bowhunters who do hunt with their target bows. I also know of some target bows that are worthy of the treestand or mountainside. Based on the logic of the preceding several paragraphs, the most forgiving hunting bow would be a target bow right off the line of the Las Vegas indoor shoot with camo tape on the limbs. But, naturally, there are always tradeoffs. "Most forgiving" doesn't always correlate with "most accurate" under hunting conditions.

As I mentioned in the discussion about brace height, arrow speed also plays an important role in shot placement when distance is unknown. Some target bows are just too slow. Their brace heights approach 10 inches and their draw cycles are so soft and spongy it's hard to tell when you've actually started pulling the string.

Because pure target bows usually have round wheels and a high brace height, they store less energy. You will sacrifice considerable arrow speed and penetration when you shoot them at game. These slow performers are not a good choice in the woods.

No, the ultimate hunting bow isn't a target bow, but a well-considered balance among speed, energy and forgiveness. In Chapter 8, I'll get into more detail on exactly why arrow speed is so important to hunting accuracy and how to find this perfect balance.

Pure target bows are the most accurate and forgiving, but they are impractical for hunting.

CONCLUSION

You need a forgiving bow, but you also need a scorching fast bow. Unfortunately, it is impossible to have both. So, one of the challenges you will face in choosing the perfect hunting bow is finding the best tradeoff between speed and forgiveness for your style of hunting. I'll help you through these decisions in the chapters on selecting the perfect bow in Chapters 5 through 8. In the meantime, we will next look at the tools and skills you will need to become a self-sufficient bowhunter.

Chapter 3

OUTFITTING YOUR WORKBENCH

B ows are becoming more and more reliable each year, but there are still many situations when you will have to make a tweak here or there on your bow or on one of your friends' bows. If you have to rely on a bow shop, or even a friend, to make these changes for you, there is some risk that when you need help the most, the shop will be closed and your friend will be gone. It is a great goal to be completely self-sufficient. If you are a serious bowhunter, and you probably are or you wouldn't have bought this book, it is more than a goal. It is a requirement.

If you are equipped to work on your own bow and arrows, you can make any necessary changes and upgrades at the time they are needed. With the right equipment, you will also be better at setting up and tuning your bow. Possibly even better than the local archery shop because you can take the time to experiment and try things.

The right tools make all the difference. Fortunately, most of them aren't very expensive. The technical demands aren't all that difficult either. This is nothing like working on a car or even a chainsaw. This is more like working on a school science project. There are only a few basic things you need to know. Assembling a proper tool kit is an important first step toward making sure your bow is working when you need it.

THE BASICS

This is the minimum tool kit. If you are just getting started, or if you are a casual bowhunter who doesn't change accessories or bows very often, you will do fine with the basic kit. When I travel to hunt, I carry the basic kit. It fits into a soft case similar to those fishermen use. It weighs about four pounds with the portable bow

Understanding basic bow maintenance and repair will keep you going when the pro shop is closed or you are in a hunting camp.

press included and takes up almost no room in my luggage.

If all you own is the basic kit, you may still find yourself going to the archery shop asking for help from time to time, but you should be able to do 90 percent of the routine work. You can find most of these items at your local pro shop or from a mail order or online archery catalog.

T-square: Used for measuring and attaching nock sets or string nocking loops. (Nock sets are those small plastic-lined brass rings that crimp onto the string above the arrow's nocking position. A nocking loop is a loop of cord knotted on the string, one knot above and one knot below the arrow, that you grab with your release aid to draw the string).

Brass nock sets: You'll need a dozen of these for starters. Forget this item if you think you will always use a string nocking loop.

Eliminator button: Buy about six or eight to start. These go under the arrow's nock on the string to cushion it from the release aid if you attach your release directly to the string rather than using a string nocking loop. Again, if you don't ever plan to use anything other than a nocking loop, you don't need eliminator buttons.

Nock point pliers: A good nock plier allows you to crimp the brass nock sets into place on the bowstring. Nock pliers also allow you to remove nock sets without damaging the string. Again, you can forget this item if you plan to use only a string nocking loop.

Extra loop material: String nocking loops make sense for a lot of reasons (I'll get to these in Chapter 23), but they will eventually wear out. You should replace the loop annually. You may as well have the material on hand. You can pick it up quickly at your local archery shop. Two feet of the loop material should last many years.

Allen wrenches: You will need several sizes of Allen wrenches to adjust the settings on your sight, rest and bow limbs and to remove and replace cam modules if your bow has them. The most convenient arrangement is a multi-wrench tool that you pick up at any hardware store. This self-contained folding wrench set has all the sizes you'll need. Choose the model with sizes from .05 to ³⁄₁₆ inches.

String wax: Routine maintenance requires bowstring wax to get maximum life from strings and synthetic fiber harnesses. Several companies make good string wax that complements today's modern synthetic strand materials.

Arrow nocks: Keep a dozen replacement nocks on hand. After a summer of hard practice, replace all your nocks before hunting with the arrows. Nocks become dinged and bent and that will really throw off your hunting arrows. Buy a dozen nocks that are identical to the ones that came on your arrows. Most any archery shop can help you out here. Don't let them talk you into a substitute. Make sure they are exactly the same as the ones you are currently using so nothing changes when you replace them.

Multipurpose tool: These tools are great for a number of tasks (screwdrivers, knife, etc.). Every bowhunter should have one in their tackle box.

Odds and ends: Stock a few extra field points, some adhesive-backed moleskin for silencing your arrow shelf and rest arms and some additional rubber tubing for your peep sight (if you use tubing to turn your peep). I also carry extra sight pins and string silencers because both are prone to break or wear out.

Get help to re-serve string: No one, beginner or experienced, is immune from the need to re-serve bowstrings periodically. Even if you buy a top-of-the-line custom string, you will likely have to re-serve the center of the string before the string wears out.

And if you buy a bow with poorly made string on it, you will need to re-serve the string shortly after you buy the bow and break the string in. If the center serving on your string looks loose or is separating near the nocking point, take the bow to the archery shop to

Most of what you need for regular bow work will fit into a tackle box.

have the string re-served. As they do this job, you should watch them carefully. Ask questions and soak it all in. When they are done, buy the needed serving tool and a spool of serving material. I recommend serving material made with Spectra fiber because it is very strong and will keep your serving tight.

Get help for bow press work: Your string may stretch for the first several months. You may need to tweak the harness length when tuning a two-cam or hybrid-cam bow — even a single-cam bow. You may also need to install string silencers or twist the string to make your peep sight come back square every time. All of these tasks require a bow press. Until you are ready to buy a press, leave these tasks to someone with more experience and more tools. After a few trips to the archery shop, you will be adding this item to your Christmas list.

ADVANCED TACKLE FOR SERIOUS BOWHUNTERS

These additions to your workbench allow you to completely tune a bow, replace strings and string-mounted accessories and build your own custom arrows. Adding these tools will give you all you need to set up or repair any bow.

The Ultimate Archery Tackle Box

BASIC KIT:

Nock pliers
Brass nock sets
Spare arrow nocks
Allen wrench set
Flat metal T-square
Spare cable guard slide
String wax
Rest silencing material
String accessories (eliminator buttons, silencers, loop material, extra peep sight)
Fisherman's tackle box to store everything
Total cost: $80 - $100

ADVANCED KIT: (everything above plus the following)

String server (I like the one made by Cavalier Equipment)
Braided Fast Flight .018- to .024-inch diameter center serving
Portable bow press
Propane torch
Adhesive for attaching inserts (normal hot melt glue for aluminum arrows or low temperature hot melt glue and/or epoxy for carbon arrows)
Several sizes and styles of fletching
Glue for vanes or feathers
Fletching jig with right helical clamp
Inserts
Spare string and harnesses
Arrow squaring device
Arrow cut-off saw
Full-size bow press
Total cost: $450 to $600

String serving tool: A string serving jig allows you to do the job right. Right not only means tight, but consistently tight. Use a good serving material, as well. I use .024-inch diameter serving made of Spectra, but some of the current braided serving materials are also very good.

If you clip your release directly to the string, you should over-serve the area of contact (between the release and serving) with a layer of old string strand material. Joel Maxfield, from Mathews, recently showed me a neat trick in which he used .016-inch diameter braided serving thread for his over-serving. He tightly pulled it down into the wraps of primary serving to tighten everything up and to produce a second level of protection against the jaws of the release.

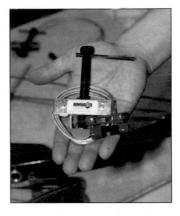

Full-size bow press: Bow presses are expensive. I tried to get by with just a portable model for several years, but with all the adjustments I was making to my bows, I soon gave in and got my hands on a full-size model. A full-size bow press is an important feature in any serious bowhunter's workshop.

A portable bow press such as the Bowmaster works fine for occasional use and travel, but if you do a lot of work on bows, you will need a full-size press eventually.

If you only work on one or two bows each year, you can probably get by with a much less expensive portable press, but you may also find that going in with a buddy on a full-size press will greatly improve your efficiency. Also, if you have the big press and don't plan to travel much to hunt, you can eliminate the expense of a portable press. Keep in mind that some of today's parallel limb bows require a specialized press that moves inward as it compresses (similar to a scissors) to accommodate the limb angle.

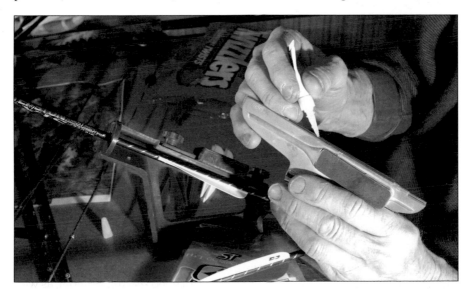

Being able to build your own arrows is a definite advantage. Not only does it save you money, it gives you that feeling of self-accomplishment.

Portable bow press: I travel with my portable press, but unless you do a lot of bow work, a portable press may be all you need at home too. Again, make sure the press you choose will work with the bow you own, be it split limb or parallel limb.

Arrow squaring device: I spin all my hunting arrows on my palm before putting them in my quiver. Not all of them spin true at first, so I use an arrow squaring device to touch up the front of each arrow and square it up with the center line of the arrow. This consistently improves the alignment of the broadheads to the arrows so they spin much better. I use it on every arrow I make.

Arrow building supplies: Get yourself a simple fletching jig with a right wing helical fletching clamp (there are many on the market). Buy the brand of fletching adhesive that corresponds with the make of fletching you use. This assures they will be compatible. I use only specialized super-glue style (cyanoacrylate) adhesives with plastic vanes. They dry fast, and I can fletch a dozen arrows in about 20 minutes.

Today's super short, rigid fletchings are impressive. If you want to be conservative, stick with four-inch vanes (or feathers if you release with fingers). If you prefer feather fletching and have a right wing clamp, be sure to buy right wing feathers. I'll spend a lot more time getting into the subject of fletching selection in Chapter 19.

To complete the arrow-building job you'll also need to cut your arrows. You can look in mail order catalogs or the Internet to find a good, simple arrow cut-off saw. They cost roughly $90. You can take all your arrows to the archery shop and pay them to cut them off, or you and a buddy can pool your money and buy a decent cut-off saw so you'll always have it when you need it.

The basic kit will cost you about $100, and you'll add another $450 to $600 for the advanced gear (maybe a bit more if you get extravagant on the fletching jig and cut-off saw). With these tools in your shop, there is no problem you can't fix.

LOOKING AHEAD

In the next chapter, I will get into the simple mechanical skills you will need to put all these tools to work for you. It is an exciting part of the journey, because now it is finally time to roll up your sleeves and start turning wrenches.

Chapter 4

MECHANICAL SKILLS FOR EVERY ARCHER

Y ou can do this. There are only a few things you need to know how to do to keep your bow working great all season.

The ability to perform routine maintenance and upgrades will make you a better bowhunter. By learning to do the work yourself, you not only are able to head off problems, but you can tweak your bow a little bit here and there to match your exact shooting style and hunting goals. This freedom to experiment will make you more accurate. Here are eight skills you can and should master before next season.

Relaxing the tension on your string and harnesses: To be truly self-sufficient, you must find a way to relax the tension on your string and harness system when necessary. You need a bow press, either a portable or a full-sized model. I recommend the full-sized model. If you can get a couple of friends to go in on it with you, these devices are reasonably affordable and they make bow work much easier and faster.

You can also simply go to the archery shop for all your bow press needs, but that defeats the goal of being self-sufficient. Not the best solution. It is far better to buy a bow press and learn to use it.

Check and set cam timing: Cam timing is a factor on all bows, but it is critical on two-cam bows. Even single-cam and hybrid cam bows require that their power cable be the correct length (within a range) to shoot properly. They aren't as sensitive to harness stretch and cam rotation as two-cam bows are, but it is still a possible issue.

The starting cam rotation (at brace) of your single-cam bow (determined by string stretch or control cable length) will affect arrow flight.

When a two-cam bow is properly timed, the eccentrics roll over at exactly the same instant. Timing is determined by the length of the cables (sometimes called harnesses). Most bows will shoot best with the timing set so that the eccentrics reach their full draw position (defined as the point where the harnesses hit the ends of their tracks) at the same time. You can actually see this by comparing the ends of the harness track as you draw the bow.

Timing discrepancies produce vertical paper tears you can't eliminate by moving the nock point up or down. If you notice that one of your cams is getting to full draw before the other, add twists to the harness attached to the cam that gets to its full draw position first. Usually, just one or two twists will make a noticeable difference.

Timing means something slightly different with a single-cam and hybrid cam bow. In both cases, timing relates to the position of the cam when the bow is at rest. Every cam has a sweet spot (an initial starting point) where it performs best. The bow will be fastest, most efficient and produce the best nock travel when it starts from this point. Several companies actually mark their cams so you can easily see if they are properly positioned to produce level nock travel and maximum efficiency.

If the single cam or hybrid cams on your bow aren't marked this way, it is a good idea to call the customer service department at your bow company and ask the representative where the cam should start (initial rotation) to perform best. Once you know this, you can easily shorten or lengthen the control cable slightly to adjust the cam rotation. The control cable is the one that anchors on the opposite limb axle and not the one that anchors on the opposite cam (or in the case of a single cam, circles the idler and becomes the bowstring).

You will need to relax the tension on the string and harness before you can adjust timing or initial cam rotation.

Adjusting draw length: Not every bow permits draw length adjustment. Some use a separate cam for every draw length with no leeway. They do this to create the best possible efficiency and nock travel (the up and down route the string's nock point takes when the arrow moves forward). But for those bows that do permit draw length adjustment, the method varies depending on the bow.

The most common method is to either turn or remove and replace (depending on cam design) the module(s). You need only an Allen wrench for this work —

you don't have to relax the string and harness tension, so no bow press is required for this change. This is very straightforward. If the bow has removable modules, you will need to purchase the correct one for the draw length you desire before you start.

If your bow doesn't have modules, it may have two or three draw-length adjustment posts that allow you to move the end of your string from one post to the other to change the bow's draw length. When you move it in a direction that makes the string act longer, you increase your draw length and when you move it in a direction that makes the string act shorter, you shorten your draw length. Generally, such an adjustment will result in a half-inch draw length change.

You will need a bow press to make this kind of a draw length change. Also, be sure to reposition your nocking point

Draw lengths are changed with a modular cam using an Allen wrench. Some cams have rotating modules while others require you to remove and replace the module with one of a different size.

on the bowstring since it will likely move as a result of the adjustment.

Re-serve your string: Factory installed bowstring center serving is notorious for becoming loose and then separating. After shooting a bow with the original serving for 200 shots, take a look at it. Replace your serving if it shows any signs of separating.

It is easy to re-serve your own string. Do so whenever the serving shows signs of separation or wear. If you shoot often, you will probably have to re-serve every year. If not, you may get by for two or even three years between serving jobs. This is very important bow maintenance and not something you can afford to take for granted. If your center serving moves during the season, you will miss an important shot.

A small hand-held string server and serving material is all that's required. Apply the serving as tightly as possible. I'm going to attempt to walk you through the serving process, but it is really quite simple. You just wind it on — do it whatever way makes the most sense to you. However, there are two absolutes. First, it has to be tight, and second, you need to wrap the serving on in the direction of the twists in the string.

To start, split the string. If the string is very tight or has a lot of twists in it, you will need to use a bow press to relax the tension so you can get the tag end of the serving material through. I always start from the top and serve down so I can keep the serving very tight at the top. It is always a bit looser where you tie it off upon completion.

After pulling about four or five inches of serving material through the middle of the string, you can take it out of the bow press. I use a couple of spare bow-strings to tie the harnesses toward the riser to get them out of the way of the serving jig. Begin turning the serving jig around the string as you wrap tightly down the string over the three inches of tag end. The wraps will naturally lay side by side, as you rotate the jig around the string. The key is to make sure the serving is tight. That is why I like Spectra serving, because it has a very high tensile strength and I can get it very tight.

Make sure you wrap the serving on the string in the direction the string is twisted. Every string has twists in it. If the twists are counter-clockwise, make sure to apply the center serving in the counter-clockwise direction.

Wrap on five or six turns and then pull the tag end of the serving material out of the way so you don't serve over it any farther. You will need that tag end later to make sure the serving bundle is super tight.

Serve your way down to the point where the other serving ended. Just before getting to the end, set up to tie it off. The easiest way to complete tie-off is to use a strand of material from an old string or a piece of heavy thread, possibly even a 10-inch piece of serving material. Make a loop with this extra material and lay it down on the string. Loosely serve over the top of the loop.

Once you have applied about six wraps on the loop, pull about five inches out of the serving jig, cut the serving off and feed the loose end through the loop. Simply pull the loop under the final six wraps, drawing the end of the serving with it.

I then tie a couple knots in the loose ends of serving material where I started and where I finished (both ends) and use pliers to pull the loose ends very tightly. Then simply trim them off flush with the wraps and you are done — a perfect custom serving job that is probably better than what they did at the factory.

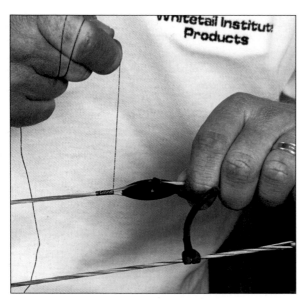

Installing a peep sight: I'm going to tell you how you can do away with rubber peep sight tubing. Use your bow press to install a conventional peep as closely as possible to the center of your bowstring. Most modern strings are made of two-tone construction so it is very easy to find the center — simply separate the colors.

Serving in a peep sight is very simple work. A bow-press and serving material will be needed.

This is an important step because it will keep the peep from turning excessively.

Move the peep up or down to position it directly in front of your eye at full draw. Tie it in place above and below using string serving material and the same basic method used for serving a string (do it by hand without a jig) and then shoot the bow at least 20 times to set the string.

If the peep isn't coming back square to your eye, relax the tension on the string and remove one end of the string from the nearest cam and add a twist or two or three to the string. When letting the press back down, make sure that the string and harnesses are in their tracks.

Take the bow out of the press and draw it several times. Shoot a few arrows through it. If you use a string nocking loop, you will probably have to move the loop around the string to keep it pointing toward the rear. Eventually, by adding one or two twists (or half twists) at a time, you will arrive at the position that brings the peep back perfectly every single time.

Even if you prefer to use the rubber tubing just for added insurance against a peep sight problem while hunting, you should still follow these steps so you can start with the peep sight in the square position so the tubing doesn't have to work so hard to bring the peep into line.

Fletching your own arrows: The first item you'll need is a fletching jig. There are several models on the market, ranging in price from around $35 up to $75, or more. If you want to buy just one fletching clamp, go with the right helical clamp. This is the most common fletching orientation. If you are using feathers, you have to buy right wing feathers to match your clamp.

Most of today's bowhunters are using four-inch fletching, but if you plan to shoot fixed blade broadheads it would be a good idea to test a few arrows with five-inch fletching, as well. You will need a separate adhesive for feather fletching than you will for plastic vanes. Typically, feather shooters use Bohning Fast Fletch and vane shooters use fast setting super glue adhesives. Clean the bases of the vanes and the shaft thoroughly with denatured alcohol. If you take the prep work seriously, you will get a bond that you literally can't tear free.

Three vanes with aggressive helical is the best choice

Learn to fletch your own arrows so you have the ability to experiment easily with different sizes and styles.

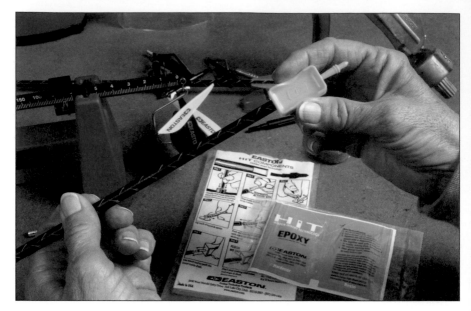

Inserts must fit properly or the broadhead will not line up perfectly with the shaft. Learn to control this important aspect of arrow building.

for most bowhunters. You can adjust the magnets on the fletching jig so that the fletching clamp changes angles. Set the clamp so that it is offset as much as possible while still getting good contact between the fletching and shaft over the full length of the fletching.

Installing and aligning inserts: It is critical to accuracy with broadheads (both mechanical and fixed-blade) that your inserts be perfectly in line with your shafts. You can test alignment by spinning the arrow while resting the tip of the broadhead on the palm of your hand, but be careful not to cut yourself with the sharp broadhead. If you feel any vibration at all, it is not perfectly aligned. You can also construct a crude turning fixture by notching two sides of a shoebox and resting the arrow in this cradle as you turn it. Compare the tip of the broadhead to a fixed reference mark. If it describes a circle, the insert is not aligned properly.

It is easy to fix inserts installed in aluminum and aluminum/carbon arrows by simply heating a field point installed in the insert until the hot melt glue holding the insert melts. Turn the tip slowly with a pair of pliers until you feel like you've floated the insert to the very center of the shaft. You can also replace your inserts with better ones that have a light press fit with the inside of the shaft.

When working with all-carbon arrows, you will find most of the inserts are glued in place. Replacing them can be destructive to the arrows themselves. In that case, your best course of action is to cull out the best arrows for hunting and use the rest for target practice. You can also improve alignment on carbon arrows by using an arrow squaring device that shaves the end of the arrow (or the end of the insert) to assure that it is perpendicular to the centerline of the shaft. I do this on every arrow I make.

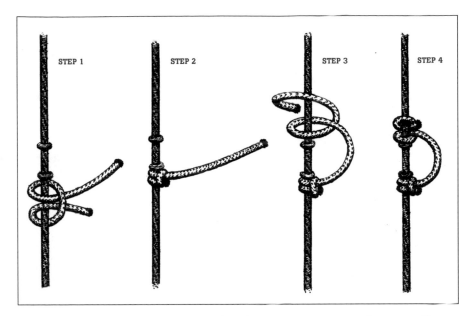

String loop tying is easy to learn and at the same time, easy to do wrong. Shown above is the proper technique. After finishing your top knot, put on your release and attach it to the loop. Pull tight to tighten the knots and to secure the string loop to the string.

Tying a string nocking loop: The loop cord is tied above and below the arrow's nock, snug to the arrow. When properly tied, you don't need to do anything else to lock the loop or the arrow in place. Cut pieces of loop cord to varying lengths and experiment to determine the best length for you and your release aid. I cut mine off at roughly 4.5 inches. Fray the ends of the cord until the fibers spread out to about the size of a dime. Then melt these loose fibers to form a ball at each end.

The finished length of my loop cords is about four inches after melting the fibers to form balls. I form good-sized balls so they won't pull through the knot when I am done tying them in place. I shoot these loops at over 85 pounds and have never had one pull through.

It is important to tie the top knot on one side of the string and the bottom knot on the other to keep the string stable and balanced during the draw. Refer to the adjacent photo for the best instructions on how to tie the knots.

Most archery shops and mail order archery companies sell loop cord. This specialized cord material is stiffer than most cording to hold its shape, making hook-ups with the release easier. It won't stretch nearly as much as other cord materials I've tried.

Don't leave important maintenance decisions up to the whim of the archery shop technician or the schedule of a buddy. If you are a serious bowhunter, it pays to learn to do the most basic work yourself. Heed the old saying: "If you want it done right, do it yourself."

LOOKING AHEAD

Now it is time to get into the important choices you must make when selecting the perfect bow for your hunting. In the next several chapters, I will go through these tradeoffs and help you select the perfect tool for filling your freezer.

Chapter 5

THE PROPER FIT FOR YOUR BOW

W hen fitting a bow to your frame, draw length and draw weight are the two most important things to consider.

EYE DOMINANCE

The first step in choosing a bow is to determine which of your eyes is dominant. A simple test will reveal this. First, with both eyes open, casually point at something specific across the room. Now, without moving your hand, first close your left eye. Then open it and close just your right eye. If the finger continues to point at the target when your right eye is open and your left eye is closed, you are right eye dominant. If it continues to aim at the target when your left eye is open and your right eye is closed, you are left eye dominant.

Ideally, you will shoot a bow that

Regardless of what hand you throw, eat or write with, you need to find your dominant eye. If you're experienced or able to shoot with your less dominant eye, then continue to do so; just concentrate on keeping the non-aiming eye closed.

fits your eye dominance. For example, if you are right eye dominant, ideally you will shoot a right-handed bow. Left eye dominant individuals should shoot a left-handed bow. The only exception to this occurs if you have already become

Body position is key to consistent accuracy. While at full draw, the forearm of your release arm should line up with your arrow and point directly back away from the target.

adept at shooting a bow with the "wrong" hand. In that case, you may as well not change. Simply shoot the bow with your dominant eye closed tightly so you don't confuse the sight picture when aiming. If you are struggling to make this work, consider changing to an opposite handed bow.

DRAW LENGTH

The draw length of the bow will determine your body position at full draw. Correct body position produces consistent accuracy, so this step is important. When aiming at full draw, the forearm of your release arm (the one holding the string back) should line up with the arrow. The elbow should point straight back away from the target.

Ask someone to stand behind you when you are fitting the bow. As you aim at the target using the release aid you will hunt with (attach a nocking loop if you will use one), have that person monitor where your elbow is pointing. If it is pointing too far to the right (for a right-handed shooter) the draw length is too short. If it is pointing too far to the left (again, reverse for left-hander) the draw length is too long.

You will find that this exercise forces you to arrive at the correct anchor point with your body relaxed and your chest expanded (not collapsed). In my experience, this will lead you to anchor with the large knuckles of your release hand back by the corner of your jawbone. If you are releasing the string with your fingers, this will bring your anchor point back along your jaw line, below and slightly behind the corner of your mouth.

Another mistake people make when establishing their anchor point is turning their heads too far away from the target in order to stretch their draw length. This promotes poor shooting form; you should avoid this bad habit. Instead, face straight at the target so you are looking out of the middle of your eyes rather than out of the corners of your eyes.

DRAW WEIGHT

For a few years, back in the early '90s, I shot a 95-pound bow. I was young and bull-headed and obviously in better shape than now. On cold days on stand, I was literally afraid a shooter buck might come past because then I would have to draw, and I thought I might pull a muscle or injure my rotator cuff. I am not shooting a 95-pound bow anymore. I gave that up within a couple of years, but I always tried to maintain my maximum at 80 pounds. It was a point of pride, like trying to squeeze into those

Attempting to shoot a bow with a draw weight that is too high will create bad habits and poor accuracy.

pants with the 34-inch waist because I didn't want to admit I had become a 36.

I remember when Joel Maxfield, at Mathews, said, "No one needs to shoot more than 70 pounds." I thought he was crazy then; now I am starting to agree with him. It is a matter of perspective and experience.

Today's new bows produce excellent efficiency. They convert draw force into arrow speed better than any we have shot in the past. That means you are getting more for less — more speed and kinetic energy for less draw force exerted.

Joel was right — for North American big game, you don't need more than 70 pounds. If you are clinging to the old hope of hauling the string back on your monster bow until you reach 60, it might be time to swallow your pride. Buy a better (more efficient) bow, drop the draw weight a bit, choose slightly lighter arrows to get the speed back up and then live with the fact you can no longer arm wrestle a gorilla without losing the arm.

You will shoot more accurately if you are not struggling to hold the string back while aiming. This applies if you are currently struggling with 80 pounds or 60 pounds. The struggle is the problem, not the exact draw weight. If you can't fully relax, you are shooting too much weight, period.

Now I need to offer a balance to keep everyone from running out and buying a 50 pounder when they can easily handle a 70 pounder. While fighting the bow is no good, there are still reasons why a stouter bow will increase your odds each fall. This is kind of a convoluted path, so stick with me. The reasoning is especially important if you are primarily a deer hunter.

Whitetails are small enough that you stand a decent chance of killing them with a shoulder hit if you are geared up for it. The shoulder and meat of the front leg are not far from the ideal aiming point — only a few inches. So, if you pull the shot a little and get into the leg, you need the best penetration you can bring to the table in order to assure you will also bring the deer to the table.

One way to increase penetration is to shoot a higher draw weight and heavier arrows. Doing so, you can expect to increase your penetration by nearly 2 percent per pound of draw force increase (as long as you also increase your arrow weight slightly). For a 10 pound increase in draw weight, you increase your penetration by nearly 20 percent. That is certainly significant. With deer-sized game, that might be enough to change the outcome of your season.

That is why I still tell everyone to shoot the most draw weight they can handle accurately. Of course, I then have to define what I mean by "handle accurately." This is the maximum draw force at which you aren't going to shoot better by reducing the draw weight but you are going to shoot worse by increasing it.

The author feels you should be able to draw your bow comfortably without any excess movement while sitting on the ground with your legs in front of you. If you can't, drop your poundage.

Here are a couple guidelines to help you find your ideal draw weight. First, make sure you can hold the string back for at least a minute without noticeable shaking. After holding the bow for this long, can you still relax and hold the pin steady when aiming? If so, you are fine; you might even try bumping up the weight a little and repeating the test.

Second, make sure you can draw the bow back without having to raise your bow arm high into the air and bring it down as you draw the string. This is a bad habit that some bowhunters get into, generally because they started with a bow they couldn't handle and then developed the wrong muscles over time.

You should be able to hold your arm out straight and draw the string back without any lurching motion. You should also be able to draw the bow while sitting flat on the ground, with your feet out in front of you. If you can't, the bow is too heavy for awkward hunting situations.

LOOKING AHEAD

When you have finally settled on the correct draw length and draw weight, there are still decisions to make. Now you must narrow the search down to a single bow model. That is where the journey takes us next: selecting the proper cam style.

Chapter 6

CAM STYLES AND LETOFF

rior to the mid-1990s, there was only one cam style on the market: dual cams. Around 1995, Mathews introduced the single cam and shortly thereafter Darton Archery introduced the first hybrid cam. Today there are four basic cam styles on the market: two cam, single cam, hybrid cam and a combination of the two cam and hybrid called the modified hybrid cam or binary cam. I'll tell you a little about each style and some of their tradeoffs.

CAM STYLES

Two-cam systems: Two-cam bows became a problem when their designs started to become aggressive. When that happened, the cams became very sensitive to synchronization problems. In other words, if one harness was made a tiny bit longer than the other or stretched slightly more after assembly, the cams didn't turn over at the same time and this resulted in poor arrow flight — a tail-high or tail-low arrow flight that was impossible to eliminate by moving the rest and nocking point.

If you checked your timing every couple of days and kept a bow press handy, you could keep these high-performance two-cam bows working fine, but you had to really watch them closely. One hot day in the back seat of the car and the synthetics making up the string and harnesses have the chance of getting cooked. The wax between the fibers can melt out and everything stretches.

I remember arriving at a Colorado elk camp after driving 22 hours in my old Cherokee. Both my bows were in a black hard case in the back of the Jeep, and the sun beat on them for many hours. When I pulled the bows out in camp, I was shocked. The cam timing was a mile off on both bows. Fortunately, I had a bow press with me, but that was the reality of the day. Those fast, high letoff two-cam bows were a handful to keep shooting well.

By the way, modern synthetics are sufficiently improved and stretch-proof that some bow manufacturers are once again making aggressive two-cam bows, and this time around, they work much better.

Most archers didn't want to be bothered with a bow that could go out of synchronization at any time, but they still wanted to shoot a fast arrow. That is why the single-cam style entered the market and became so popular — it solved this problem.

Single-cam system: The top limb of a single-cam bow carries an idler wheel and the bottom limb carries the cam. The idler wheel provides no mechanical advantage; it is simply there to unroll the string as you draw the bow. The bottom cam does two things, it takes up the control cable as you draw the string (this is what flexes the limb tips toward each other) while at the same time letting out the other end of the string at the correct rate to keep the nock travel-

Single-cam bow at full draw; note cam at the bottom and round idler wheel at the top.

ing straight back and straight forward.

The single cam is not sensitive to changes in power cable length. If the power cable stretches a little, the bow remains in tune because there is only one cam.

Hybrid-cam systems: You can think of hybrid cams as a mix of single-cam and two-cam technology. They do about the same thing as a single-cam bow. In other words, because the top cam is attached directly to the bottom cam (the top cam is called the slave and the bottom cam is called the master) these systems are less sensitive to power cable stretch. When the power cable stretches, both cams move instead of just one, as is the case of the two-cam bow. Therefore, hybrid cams are more reliable than two-cam bows because they are much less sensitive to timing issues.

A smooth drawing bow is an advantage in a treestand, but you give up speed to get smoothness. It is a trade-off.

Hybrid cams are supposed to make it easier to attain perfectly level nock travel. This is important for good arrow flight. Not all bows produce perfect nock travel. That means some bows are easier to tune than others, and some can't be tuned at all. I'll dig into the important subject of nock travel in the next chapter.

It is debatable whether the hybrid has any tuning advantages over a well-made single cam. This system is certainly better than poorly made single cams I have shot. I have endured some amazingly bad arrow flight from single-cam bows whose cams were not properly designed for all draw lengths. I think if these poorly made single cams had been effectively policed off the market by some licensing agreement, the hybrid never would have gained traction. Instead, people began blaming all single cams for the problems of only a few.

Hybrid-cam system. Note that both cams are eccentric in shape. However, they differ from a two-cam system because they are tied together.

Regardless of why it became popular, the hybrid is now a big part of the bow landscape. Most bow companies have some form of hybrid cam. If you have a non-standard draw length like me (mine is 32 inches), you will benefit from a hybrid cam because all but a very few single cams produce poor arrow flight at the extremes of the draw length range.

The only single-cam bows that didn't produce poor arrow flight for me were those that didn't rely on modules. These bows feature a separate cam for every draw length. If I were buying a single-cam bow right now, I would certainly lean toward these specialized bows.

Modified hybrid-cam systems: Modified hybrids are the newest style on the market. Some companies call them binary cams. The top and bottom cams are mirror images of each other. Rather than the harness attaching to the opposite limb tip, it attaches to the opposite cam. In this way, the cams are slaved together just as they are with a standard hybrid cam, but the harness tracks and string payout tracks are identical on top and bottom, making it very easy to produce level nock travel.

The biggest difference between the hybrid and the modified hybrid cam is

Note the tuning marks scribed into the cam. This is one way manufacturers help you determine the correct cam rotation when tuning.

the fact that there is no set slave and master. It changes depending on the lengths of the harnesses. All that matters is the fact that the cams are linked together so they can't change rotation independently and go out of time.

To summarize, I don't recommend a two-cam bow. There is not enough to gain from that design that it is worth the nagging problem of always having to check cam timing. Select a single cam, hybrid cam or a modified hybrid cam style. However, just to be on the safe side, don't walk out of the archery shop until you know the bow you have selected can be tuned. More about tuning in Chapters 26 through Chapter 31.

HARD VERSUS SOFT CAMS

The shape of the cam and the way it loads the limbs of your bow will have a big affect on how the bow feels when you draw the string and how fast it shoots an arrow. Most of the hunting bows on the market today are equipped with what I would classify as hard or medium cams and they all tend to have high letoff, between 70 and 80 percent. In this next section, I'm going to tell you why it matters, how to read a force versus draw curve and how to interpret letoff numbers.

WHY IT MATTERS

Comfort is important when shooting a bow. You have to feel comfortable while drawing and holding the string so you can relax and take steady aim. That is one reason the feel of the draw is important. Some bowhunters don't like the feel of an aggressive hard cam bow that comes up to poundage quickly and then holds the maximum well into the draw before dropping off sharply into the letoff valley. It can feel intimidating and can create tension for some archers.

A smooth drawing bow is not as fast as an aggressive bow, but the smoothness can pay off when drawing to shoot in awkward positions.

If you hand 20 archers the same 10 bows to draw and handle, they will all prefer the smoothest one. However, when it comes time to shoot the bow at a target, when you start to factor in speed, the choices change. I've actually done this. Everyone likes a smooth bow, but when the rubber meets the road on the target range, speed starts to win out. There is a tradeoff between smooth draw and arrow speed. Typically, for reasons I'll get into in the next section, a bow that has a super smooth draw won't produce fast arrow flight.

Your body will become accustomed to the feel of any bow's draw over time. The muscles will learn when to pull hard and when to let up so the draw doesn't feel quite as clunky and harsh. However, the draw cycle of an aggressive hard cam bow will never feel smooth.

Here is my advice. If you think you will practice a lot before the season and will make a point of shooting at least three times per week during the season to stay sharp, a hard drawing, aggressive cam bow is an acceptable choice. But, if you know you won't have a lot of time to practice going into the season and won't likely shoot much once it starts, you had better stick with a smooth drawing bow.

In the treestand or ground blind, the harsh-drawing bow will be intimidating and have you playing emotional catch-up. That sets you up for a tense shot. It sounds crazy, but it is true. You have to shoot an aggressive bow consistently or it will be a little intimidating. No one needs that when drawing on a nice buck or bull.

FORCE VERSUS DRAW CURVES

You may have read somewhere about a certain bow having a smooth force versus draw curve. This is high school physics and shouldn't cause you to burn out any brain cells. If you draw a bow and measure the force it takes to pull the string back at each point along the way; and then plot those two numbers on paper (with the amount of force shown along the vertical scale and the distance shown along the horizontal scale), you have the force versus draw curve. I like to look at them because they tell me everything I need to know about how the bow will feel when

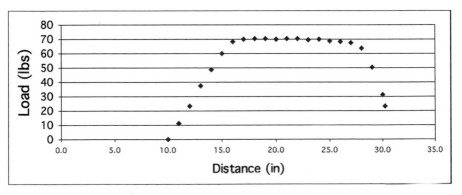

A force versus draw curve measures the force it takes to pull the string back at each point of the draw cycle. The curve then shows the amount of force along the vertical scale and the distance shown on the horizontal scale.

I draw it and how fast it will likely shoot.

The area shown under the curve is the amount of energy the bow stores. So, if a bow has a draw force that comes up to maximum poundage quickly, the curve will start out much more vertical and then have a wide flat top. That increases the amount of area under the curve for any given maximum draw weight. Likewise, if the draw force drops off sharply into a narrow letoff valley, the curve will show that, as well.

The more "square" the force vs. draw curve looks, the more clunky and harsh the draw will feel, but the faster the bow will likely shoot because it is storing more energy. This is where you see the trade-off between feel and speed.

UNDERSTANDING LETOFF

I have come to like high letoff. When the high letoff bows first came out, I continued to opt for 65 percent letoff because that lower letoff produced a faster arrow (again, it has to do with the fact that the lower letoff stores more energy). However, once I tried a 75-percent letoff bow, I would not go back to 65 percent letoff even if you gave me a lifetime supply of energy bars. I am much more comfortable at full draw with the higher letoff, which allows me to relax more and aim steadier — again, feel is very important.

Letoff is a simple thing to understand. I already touched on the subject in Chapter 1, but I'll hit it again here. Letoff is the percentage of the maximum draw weight that disappears at full draw. Lets say you shoot a 60-pound bow with 70 percent letoff. At some point in the draw, you were pulling 60 pounds. At full draw, 70 percent of that amount is gone (42 pounds). So, you are holding 18 pounds.

Bow technicians measure letoff in two ways, effective letoff and AMO standard letoff. Effective letoff is the most common number you will see when looking at the bow's specification sheet. It is measured after the bow reaches full draw and the string has eased slightly forward.

AMO standard letoff is measured at full draw, as the string is still being pulled backward. Friction always works in the opposite direction of the movement of the string. With AMO letoff, the friction is working against you, making the holding weight seem heavier. With effective letoff, the friction is working forward, attempting to hold the string back as it is inclined to go forward.

Effective letoff is always a larger number than AMO letoff. If you shoot the way you are supposed to, pulling against the back of the valley, AMO letoff is the true letoff you will feel. However, if you creep the string forward slightly while aiming, as many bowhunters are prone to do, you will be sensing the effective letoff (holding less weight).

LOOKING AHEAD

Cams are the heart and soul of your bow. They determine how the draw will feel, how long the letoff valley will be and how much weight you have to hold while aiming. They even determine whether you will be able to tune your bow and keep it tuned. But cams aren't always designed perfectly, and when they aren't, they can introduce a huge headache that will turn your bow into a lemon. I have owned a few of these. In the next chapter I'll teach you how to avoid owning a lemon.

Chapter 7

THE IMPORTANCE OF NOCK TRAVEL

I 've owned some bows that were lemons. They were impossible to tune and the reason was that they produced nock travel that was impossible to correct. Nock travel matters. It is the path taken by the nock point on the string as you draw and release the arrow. The nock can (but shouldn't) move up and down and side-to-side. Both are detrimental to your ability to tune the bow. The very best nock travel is straight back and straight forward without any sideways or vertical movement.

Delivering a straight flying arrow is the most important thing your bow has to do. When you shoot, the tail of your arrow will follow the nocking point (or nocking loop) attached to your bowstring. It has to; they are attached. If a bow doesn't produce good nock travel, it doesn't matter how fast it is or how good the grip feels — you will never tune it or shoot it to your satisfaction.

If you have tried everything and your bow just won't tune, chances are you have a nock travel problem.

OWNING LEMONS

The lemons I have owned over the years were bad because the nock point on the string moved dramatically up, down or sideways during the shot. I'm not going to name any brands (I had bad bows from 10 different companies). I remember one bow I received prior to going on a hunt with one of the top representatives from the company that sent it to me. That bow was so bad the arrow nearly went through the tuning paper sideways. I took one shot with the bow and started laughing. I knew there was no possible way I would ever shoot that thing at game. It was a joke.

I brought one of my other bows (made by a different company) along on the hunt and hid it in the back of the truck. Whenever we went out to hunt, I would sneak them both out and stash the pitiful one in the brush. I'd use my other bow and then sneak them both back into the truck again when the designated driver came back to pick me up. That was the worst bow I have ever seen, but others were nearly as bad.

Most of these bows have been weeded out, thankfully, but there are still a few lemons on the market. That's why I always recommend that you first tune any bow you are considering buying. I'll get into tuning in a later chapter.

Is nock travel important? It isn't just important; it is everything.

UP AND DOWN NOCK TRAVEL

As I mentioned in the last chapter, some of the companies making modular, single-cam bows shot very bad arrows at my draw length. I have a long draw, and I'm sure my draw length was beyond what those modular cams could handle, but there was no disclaimer on the packaging "Not Good for Draw Lengths Past 29 inches." It is a pet peeve of mine when companies produce a product that simply doesn't work, and at my draw length, those modular, single-cam bows didn't work.

Poor vertical nock travel also arises if you are shooting a two-cam bow and the cams aren't synchronized. My introduction to nock travel problems came with a two-cam bow. I had one that I couldn't tune. Then on a whim I experimented with the cam synchronization and like magic, it was fixed. That was a vertical nock travel issue, but a very easy one to fix. There is a section about timing two-cam bows in Chapter 4.

If you have a vertical nock travel problem with a single-cam or hybrid-cam bow, you will find it is much tougher to fix. You can play with cam rotation by twisting or untwisting the control cable on these bows, but that is only going to give you a little bit of adjustment. And you can move the nocking point up or down on your string, but that is just a Band-Aid that rarely fixes this problem.

If the system isn't designed well for

Your cams and idler wheel (if single cam) should line up with the string to assure that the bow will produce good arrow flight.

your draw length, you are in trouble. That was the case with those early modular single cams. They weren't good at every draw length. I'm sure there are a few out there that still aren't.

The only sure way to fix this problem is to avoid owning such a bow in the first place. Again, make sure to first tune any bow you consider buying before plunking down your hard-earned money. If the seller won't let you attempt to tune it before you buy it, look somewhere else. Any bow manufacturer that is actually selling good bows will be the first to agree. They want you to see how good their bows are because it is their strongest selling point.

SIDE-TO-SIDE NOCK TRAVEL

I had a bow one time that I had a miserable time tuning. I liked everything about it except the arrow flight. The arrow kept hitting the right hand launcher on the rest hard enough to wear away the metal while damaging the downward-pointing cock vane. No matter how much I moved the rest and tweaked the arrow's nock rotation, I couldn't make it better. I finally went to a cushion plunger rest that produces side pressure and saw a bit of improvement, but it nagged me that I had to put a Band-Aid on what was obviously a major wound.

As time went on, I started to learn more about sideways nock travel and then I went back to that bow to try to fix it again. I went through everything that can cause the problem without benefit when finally, on a hunch, I swapped out the thin riser for a beefier one from the same manufacturer. The problem instantly went away.

Now get this, the riser itself was bowing to the left — buckling — every time I drew the string and then springing back when I released the string. That is what caused the arrows to kick to the right. Who would have thought of something like that causing a nock travel problem? Obviously, the people who designed the bow didn't. Apparently, they didn't bother to test it either, or they didn't care.

Cam lean is the most common cause of sideways nock travel. If the cams change their vertical angle during the draw, and then go back to their original angle as the string moves forward, the string will travel sideways. That's not good — I'm sure you appreciate that by now. You can sight down the bowstring and quickly tell if there is a potential cam lean problem. Ideally, the cam or cams are straight in line with the string both when the bow is undrawn and

You can sometimes correct limb twist by shortening one side of the bow's split harness yoke to bring the cam or idler back in line with the string.

at full draw. If they aren't, you have the potential for problems.

Cams lean for three reasons. First, the most common reason for cam lean occurs because the forces acting on the limb tip are not balanced. The forces are higher on one side of the axle than on the other, causing the limb to twist. Some of this is just a product of the way your bow was designed and you can't do much about it. However, if the bow has a harness yoke that spans the limb tip, you might be able to twist up one side of the yoke and pull the cam back to a more balanced, vertical position.

I ran into this a couple of seasons back. A bow that had always shot like a rifle for me was throwing arrows a little sideways. I puzzled over it for a few weeks until I realized one of the cams was leaning to the side slightly. By putting a few twists in one side of the harness yoke, I pulled the limb tip around and the cam straightened right out. The bow started shooting perfectly again.

Second, cams lean if the axle holes aren't drilled at a 90-degree angle to the limbs. It would be really hard to know for sure without taking the cams off and laying a square along the limbs and axle, but if you think you may have this problem, you might be able to take the bow to a dealer for warranty repair (a new set of limbs).

Cams can also lean if the bushings that allow the cam to turn on the axles are worn out. This is less common today because many bows use bearings instead of bushings, but for bows made in the late '90s and early 2000s, it occasionally occurs.

It is very important for any serious archer to understand that nock travel is not just a nice bonus to a top-name bow — it is the only reason you buy a bow. Without level and straight nock travel, you will find it is very hard to tune your bow.

LOOKING AHEAD

Bows aren't cheap. It is very realistic for manufacturers to provide a bow that shoots perfect arrows and well within your rights as a paying consumer to expect nothing less. Another aspect of bow design will also improve your success this fall. Car salesmen say that you don't sell the steak, you sell the sizzle. Well, in the world of hunting bows, the sizzle is definitely arrow speed. In the next chapter I will take you through the reasons why I think you should be shooting a fast arrow.

Chapter 8

IMPORTANCE OF ARROW SPEED

O ther than making the bow quieter, I don't see any advantage to shooting a slow arrow. Today's bows have the quality and design required to shoot even fast arrows accurately. I have compiled the four biggest reasons why a faster arrow is a better arrow.

FLATTER TRAJECTORY

When you bring up the advantages of a faster arrow, the first thing most bowhunters think of is a bigger margin for error when estimating shot range. Fast arrows fly flatter, making it less critical that you get the range perfect when taking shots past 25 yards. At distances up to 25 yards, range estimation is not critical to your results. If you misjudge a 22-yard shot and think it is 17 yards, you will still make a good hit (maybe a bit low). But if you misjudge a 30-yard shot and think it's 35 yards, that is a completely different matter.

The farther you plan to shoot, the more accurate your range estimate must be to

A bigger margin of error is one of the biggest benefits of shooting a faster arrow, and today's rigs make shooting down range easier than ever.

produce clean kills. While arrow speed won't save a grossly wrong estimate, it will help you out when you are off by only a few yards.

You may be tempted to think you can just rely on your new rangefinder to do all the work for you. When you have the time, I agree. Range finders are awesome tools. I love mine. Unfortunately, on about 25 percent of the shots I take from a treestand, I don't have time to use my range finder. It used to be closer to 50 percent, but I have gotten better at using the range finder fast because I shoot a lot of does and I am not afraid to miss an opportunity by taking the extra few seconds required to get the range exactly right.

That means that even when making an intentional effort to use the range finder on every shot, I still have to guess the range on 25 percent of them. Sure, like most bowhunters, I have pre-ranged reference points around my stands that I can hopefully find and organize in my head, but often I panic when things happen fast and can't sort them out quickly enough. The fate of the shot comes down to my ability to judge distance simply by looking at the animal. That is when I am glad I'm shooting a fast arrow.

Your sight pins will show you your arrow's trajectory at all points in its flight. For example, for a 40-yard shot, the arrow will occupy the point in space when it is 30 yards away that is directly in line with the 30-yard pin. This helps you avoid deflections. Obviously, the narrower the pin gap, the easier it is to shoot through gaps in the cover.

By the numbers: First, I'll start with a 240 fps arrow. If you are standing on level ground and aim using your 30-yard pin, you will hit a seven-inch vital area if the actual distance is between 24.6 and 33.9 yards. The total window is 9.3 yards wide. Now if you bump the speed up to 290 fps, you will make a clean kill if the animal is actually between 20.6 and 35.5 yards away. The total window increases to 14.9 yards. That is enough to make a difference. If you have ever ricocheted an arrow off the brisket of a big buck (and I have), you know those extra couple of yards can be significant. I'll take every yard I can get.

SHOOTING THROUGH HOLES

One of my most painful misses came on a woodland caribou. I spent the whole day trying to get within bow range of the bull. I had literally crawled several miles through a bog and had gone all day without food or water. Late in the afternoon, I finally had the brute (he would have scored near the top of the record book) at 40 yards. I stumbled upon the spot where he was bedded in a small island of trees out in the middle of nowhere. My GPS said I was eight miles from where I had left my guide. The bull stood up and was just getting ready to walk off.

The only hole I could find to his vitals was down low, so I spread my legs wide to form a solid base for the shot, took aim and squeezed the trigger. The arrow arched upward and slammed into a branch above my line of sight, one that I had not even thought to look for during the few quick seconds. Goodbye bull.

I've missed three other big animals (one was a mule deer that I'm sure was over 190 inches and the other two were big whitetails) because my arrows hit branches that were above my line of sight. I have since learned to look around the sight line on every shot, but I'm sure there will still be times when the hole I want to shoot through is small. A fast arrow will pass easier through smaller holes in the brush than a slower one.

By the numbers: Let's say you are lining up to take a 40-yard shot at a nice buck that is feeding in a clover patch. You zapped him with your laser rangefinder, and you know the distance to the nearest half yard. You have practiced 40-yard shots until they are easy for you. This is a green light situation.

There is only one problem: you have to shoot through a hole in the branches of a tree that is 20 yards away. If you are shooting a 240 fps arrow, it will be on a path that takes it 12.1 inches above your line of sight when it goes through the hole (it's going to have to be a pretty big hole). If you are shooting a 290 fps arrow, it will be 8.3 inches above your line of sight when it goes through the

When shooting through gaps in the brush, a fast arrow with a flat trajectory is a benefit.

hole. That lets you shoot through a hole that is nearly four inches smaller. I think that is a big deal. In fact, I would shoot a fast arrow even if this were the only benefit I received. Happily, there is more.

STRING JUMPERS

Some deer will drop at the sound of the shot to load up their legs in order to run away. This often produces a miss or high hit. I have shot a bunch of deer (I'm a devoted doe shooter if you haven't figured that out yet) in a bunch of places and I have yet to draw a solid conclusion on the best place to aim when hunting deer that might drop at the shot.

I also have yet to figure out how much bow noise is too much and how it affects the likelihood that a deer will move before the arrow arrives. I've seen deer that turned inside out even when I was shooting a very quiet bow.

Here is why I feel arrow speed is so important when shooting at potential string jumpers. I have yet to shoot a compound so quiet that a deer can't hear it at 40 yards on a still day. Deer have better hearing than we do. However, with a little bit of wind, if another deer is walking nearby, and when hunting in thick cover, I have seen bucks and does completely miss the sound of a quiet bow. Also, they are much more likely to react if they are already alert when you shoot, eliminating any benefit you might have gotten from a quiet bow.

As far as I am concerned, it is a mixed bag. Quiet is good and fast is good; neither seems more important than the other. Actually, both are important. Unfortunately, you have to trade them off. For that reason, I think the best combination is a fast arrow (one that weighs about six to 6.5 grains per pound of draw force) from the quietest bow you can find.

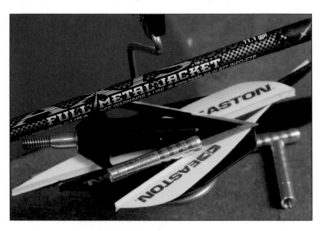

By the numbers: I recently did a study to determine how far a deer can drop between the time it hears the shot and the arrival of the arrow. Of course, a faster arrow gets there sooner so the deer doesn't drop as far. This is especially important on shots from 25 to 35 yards. At this distance, the deer is close enough to hear even a quiet bow, yet it is far enough that it can drop a good distance before the arrow arrives.

A lighter arrow will increase arrow speed. You gain roughly one foot per second for every five grain reduction in arrow weight.

I had to make a few assumptions to come up with the final numbers. For example, I estimated that it takes a deer .05 seconds to begin moving after hearing a startling sound, roughly half that of the finest human athletes. It is just a guess. Using this guess, I determined that at 30 yards from a treestand, a deer will drop roughly 16.75 inches with a 230 fps arrow. He may even have time to turn slightly. The deer will drop roughly 9.5 inches with a 280 fps arrow. That's a 7.5-inch difference!

When aiming a 230 fps arrow at a buck that appears alert, you will have to aim below the bottom of the deer's chest (16.75 inches is a long ways). It is hard to make yourself do that when you don't know for sure how the deer will react to the shot. He may drop and he may not. You will only know for sure after you release the string. I would much rather have a fast arrow and aim for the bottom of the kill zone. If he drops, I should still be in the top of the kill zone. If he only drops a little, I am dead center and if he doesn't drop at all, I am low in the kill zone. The only way you can have this luxury is to shoot a fast arrow.

At short range, string jumping isn't really a factor. Arrow speed is much less important at short range than it is at mid range and long range. For example, at 10 yards the deer drops an inch, or less, with the slower arrow and almost nothing at all with the faster arrow. It is not worth considering when aiming.

Six Ways To Increase Arrow Speed

If you are looking for every edge you can get, it makes sense to wring a few more feet per second from your bow — as long as you can do it without giving up any pure (on the shooting range) accuracy. With that in mind, here are seven ways you can turn your old dud into a real zinger.

DRAW LENGTH

If you're betting on an arrow speed contest, take the tall guy every time. All else being equal, the guy with the longest draw length will win. Though increasing your draw length brings speed advantages, you have to do it carefully. I laid out a method to determine your correct draw length in Chapter 5. Stick with those principles and you will do fine.

Increasing draw weight will increase arrow speed by roughly two feet per second per pound.

If you are shooting an aggressive cam, speed may increase as much as 3 to 3.5 percent for each inch of additional draw length. So, if you're shooting 250 fps with your current setup, and anchoring an inch short of your optimum position, you could gain as much as nine fps, not to mention the benefits of greater accuracy that come from using the correct draw length.

INCREASE YOUR POUNDAGE

If you can boost your poundage without over-burdening yourself, you'll increase both speed and penetration. Again, go back to Chapter 2 and stick with the principles of selecting your maximum draw weight. For a reasonable hunting bow, a five-pound weight increase will result in a speed improvement of about 10 fps.

CAM DESIGN

You could see a significant increase by upgrading to a more aggressive bow. Going from a round wheel bow to the most radical cam, at the same draw weight and draw length, the increase will be approximately 15 to 20 percent. That's based upon IBO standard arrow speed numbers for the different bow types. The increase from moderate cam to aggressive cam will be less, about 7 to 10 percent.

LIGHTER ARROWS

You can select full-length arrows that weigh anywhere from five grains per pound of maximum draw force to as high as 10 grains per pound of your bow's draw weight. For a 60-pound bow you can find properly spined arrows weighing anywhere from 300 to 600 grains! For every five grains of arrow weight reduction, you will see roughly one fps increase in speed. However, going below six grains of arrow weight per pound of draw force is generally considered risky because your bow will be forced to absorb a lot more vibration.

PROPERLY SPEC YOUR BOW

Your bow will perform better with the limb bolts very close to being bottomed. The amount of pre-stress on your limbs affects the shape of the draw-force curve and how much energy your bow stores when you draw it. Let's say you want to shoot 55 pounds. You can back off the limb bolts on a 70-pound bow until it registers 55 pounds or you can buy a 55-pound bow and tighten the limb bolts down. The second option will produce a lot more speed for the same poundage. A five percent speed increase is definitely not out of the question.

SMALL TWEAKS

String weight: Use a lightweight peep sight, reserve your string with a shorter section of serving and consider serving on your nock sets rather than using brass sets. Also, consider a string loop instead of heavier nock locating systems. This can produce a speed increase of about three fps.

Lubrication: Keep the wheel bushings and axles lubricated; it'll add another few fps. Also, a Teflon cable guard slide will decrease friction.

PUTTING IT ALL TOGETHER

While it can be counterproductive to worry about a few feet per second here and there — you'll never notice the difference — it is worth your time and effort if you can add 10 or 20 percent to your arrow speed. When done carefully, in a way that doesn't detract from your accuracy, you'll definitely become more effective when taking shots beyond 25 yards.

MORE KINETIC ENERGY

As long as you keep the same arrow weight, making it go faster increases the punch it packs when it lands. Most experts agree that kinetic energy is the best measure of the penetration ability of an arrow. Heavier arrows will soak up more of the energy from your bow and that translates into more kinetic energy. However, you can also increase kinetic energy by shooting the same arrow faster.

You will get better performance for any given draw weight if you shoot a bow designed to produce that weight with the limbs bottomed, or close to bottomed.

There are some very fast bows on the market now. If you are shooting a bow with an IBO speed rating of 300 to 305 fps, you are shooting a bow with average speed. There are now bows producing IBO speeds in excess of 320 fps with forgiving brace heights and comfortable draw cycles. In that way, technology has definitely improved the performance of modern bows.

By the numbers: You can calculate kinetic energy using the following equation: KE = total arrow grain weight divided by 450,240 and then multiplied by the arrow velocity in fps squared. Assume you shoot a 450-grain arrow at 240 fps. Your KE is 58 foot pounds of energy. Now, if you can bump your arrow speed up to 290 fps with the same arrow, your KE goes to 84 foot pounds. Shooting the same arrow out of a faster bow will increase your penetration energy by 45 percent!

Granted, you probably won't make the full 50 fps improvement simply by changing to a faster bow, but even if you improve your energy by 30 percent, or even 25 percent, you are making a significant difference.

Arrow speed is still a very important part of the overall success equation. I know bowhunters who would not ever consider hunting with a bow shooting less than 300 fps. I generally shoot around 285 to 290 fps. There are many reasons why this makes sense to me. The only downside is a slightly noisier bow, and with the strides that have been made by bow companies in recent years to make their bows quieter (and with all the aftermarket accessories), my bows are much quieter today than they were 10 years ago. If you choose the right bow, you can realistically expect to shoot fast and quiet. Get the best of both worlds.

LOOKING AHEAD

In the next chapter I am going to get into the subject of draw length consistency in a little bit more detail. It is not a long chapter, but I think you will find it eye-opening.

Chapter 9

DRAW LENGTH FORGIVENESS

T he ideal anchor point is one you can repeat. This may be the most overlooked part of setting up and accurately shooting a bow. Most bowhunters
have a range in which they anchor — that is not a good thing. They may
use a peep sight to lock in the vertical position, but there is still nothing to lock in
the distance they draw the string. Some bows have a wide valley and soft back

wall, and it would be easy with such a
bow to vary your draw length by as much
as a half inch.

On some days, you may pull the string
solidly into the back wall. On other days,
when you are tired or under pressure,
you may collapse slightly and creep into
the middle of the letoff valley instead.
Such a small change in form doesn't seem
like a big deal. Most bowhunters would
not even consider it a flaw, but it has
serious consequences. On the worst bows,
only a half inch change in anchor point
(draw length) will cause your arrows to
hit as much as four inches off target at
just 20 yards. Even most of the best bows
will be off at least two inches at that
range if you vary your draw length by
a half inch.

*If your anchor point moves forward,
or you creep the arrow forward by col-
lapsing your form, it may cause large
fluctuations in impact location.*

When you pull the string back slightly farther or shorter than normal, you change the relationship between your eye, the pin and the target. When you vary the draw length, the riser tips. The arrow doesn't follow the sight up or down on the target. It has to do with the geometry of a bow.

Next time you are practicing, pay particular attention to exactly how you anchor. Unless you are a highly skilled competitive shooter, I bet you'll be surprised by how much your draw length fluctuates.

ARRIVING AT YOUR ANCHOR POINT

The way you reach your anchor point also affects your consistency — even if you end up at the same draw length every time. You can either pull back to your anchor point and then shoot while maintaining tension on the string at that point or you can pull past your anchor point and then ease (creep) forward to the same location. If you alternate between these two methods, you will see larger groups than if you hold strictly to just one style. At 20 yards, the difference can be as much as 1.5 inches.

ALL BOWS ARE NOT CREATED EQUAL

You can sight in every bow on the market and put them into a shooting machine, but they will not all shoot the same. A bow's ability to forgive changes in draw length is part of its design.

Using a shooting machine, you can make all bows shoot arrow after arrow into the same hole even at 20 yards. But problems arise when things change from one shot to the next. Any changes in draw length, in particular, without re-sighting the bow can result in major accuracy problems.

This brings up another important point. Some bows suffer from string stretch that occurs after the bow is sighted in. Most bowhunters just live with one half

When buying a new bow, ask about the quality of the harness and draw the bow back to check the back of the anchor point. A solid back wall is key to a repeatable, consistent anchor point and accuracy.

Lessons From A Shooting Machine

The best shooters have learned through actual shooting the same things that Steve Johnson, maker of the Hooter Shooter shooting machine, has learned through extensive testing. How far you pull the string makes a huge difference in impact.

"We've tested many bows by using the machine to draw them back various distances within what we feel is a reasonable error range for many bowhunters," Steve said. "Assuming that's about a one half-inch range, we found that some bows are much more critical of this slight change than others. As we varied the draw length, the worst bow we tested had an impact that moved more than four inches on a target located only 20 yards away. Most bows were off by at least two inches."

A shooting machine like Spot-Hogg's Hooter Shooter teaches lessons that are harder to see when shooting the bow by hand. Varying your anchor point by just one-half inch can throw your arrows off by two to four inches.

Johnson further stated that he was able to "fix" the bow with the four-inch error by simply changing the bow's timing (it was a two-cam bow). When it was timed perfectly, the bow was very unforgiving of changes in draw length. However, when the top cam was set to arrive at full draw slightly ahead of the bottom cam the bow adjusted automatically and the pin followed the impact point perfectly. "In most cases we set two-cam bows so that the harness attached to the bottom cam is about one twist shorter than the top one," Johnson said. "Also, by going to a sight with a longer extension bar you can make your bow more forgiving of changes in draw length.

"With single-cam bows we use a string held taut between the axles to provide a reference for measuring tiller. We first set the tiller equal and then experiment until the bow's impact tracks the sight through small changes in draw length and anchor point. This procedure is most quickly accomplished with a shooting machine because all human errors are eliminated. You know immediately after making a change whether the bow is more or less forgiving."

There is an important lesson here: never take your anchor point and draw length for granted. After learning these lessons from Johnson and applying them to my own shooting, I have begun to shoot more consistently. I have also made it a rule that I will only shoot bows with rock solid back walls that I can pull against. This gives me a solid reference that allows me to be much more consistent than I could ever be shooting a bow with a soft back wall.

inch of extra draw length rather than fight it, but they will not be as accurate as they were when the bow had the proper length string.

Zero stretch, zero twist custom strings may seem an expensive option on the surface, but good ones will eliminate most of the problems associated with stretch. I use them for that reason. When buying a new bow, make sure it has a good string and harnesses or put a new set on your Christmas list for your existing bow.

Accuracy depends entirely on consistency. If you do exactly the same thing every single time you shoot your bow, you will do just fine even if your method is less than textbook. However, when you change your form even slightly, problems arise. This is never truer than when anchoring for the shot — your draw length must be the same every time.

As I mentioned in Chapter 2, it is very hard to know when you buy a bow if it will be forgiving of changes in draw length. In fact, unless you have a shooting machine right there to test the bow (and a lot of experience), you are completely in the dark.

However, you can take a simple step to help assure that your bow will be consistent. If the bow has a solid back wall at full draw (whether through cam design or the use of a draw stop on the cam), you can be sure that at least your draw length will be consistent The bow doesn't have to be forgiving of draw length changes if your draw length never changes. Keep that in mind when buying a new bow or setting up your existing bow. A super solid back wall is the only way to go.

LOOKING AHEAD

There isn't a lot of debate in the matter of maintaining a consistent anchor point and a consistent draw length, but in the next chapter I'll take on the trend toward short bows. While there are situations in which a short bow will improve your success rate, the trend is completely overdone. Short bows are not as stable as longer bows and thus they aren't as forgiving. Turn the page and we will start into the subject of bow length.

Chapter 10

SHOOTING SHORT BOWS

I t wasn't many years ago that long axle-to-axle bows were supposed to be better. Target shooters opted for the longest bows they could find. They added weights near the limb pockets; some even melted lead and poured it into the voids inside the pockets themselves. This reasoning was easy to understand; the extra length and weight made the bows more stable. Now, all of a sudden, shorter is better. It would be nice to know what is fact and what is fiction.

MAKING A BOW THAT'S HARD TO MOVE

Newton's Law states: Force equals mass times acceleration. The greater the inertia (or mass) of the body, the harder it is to accelerate. You may have heard a physics or science teacher once state: A body at rest wants to remain at rest. My evenings on the sofa in front of the television can vouch for this simple truth.

This means that longer and heavier objects are harder to move quickly than shorter or lighter objects. That plastic baseball bat you had when you were six was a lot easier to accelerate than

Stability comes from three factors: weight, length and the number (and length) of stabilizers you use.

the wooden version your Major League heroes were swinging.

When shooting a bow, there are hundreds of ways you can ruin a shot, but they all fall into just a few categories. One category is torque. You can torque a bow by tipping it side-to-side, along the axis of your bow arm. That would be the motion you have when you rotate your forearm. Or, you can also torque the bow by turning it from left to right, along the axis running from axle-to-axle on the bow. That would be the motion you have when you hinge and unhinge your wrist.

A long bow (axle-to-axle length) is more stable than a shorter bow and one reason you typically find longer bows in the target arena.

A long bow resists rotation around the axis that runs through your bow arm. Think about it. If you grab the grip during the shot, the longer bow is not going to be as easy to move as a shorter, lighter bow. Here is another way to look at this. Which would be easier to rotate quickly when held at arm's length, a six-foot long steel bar that weighs four pounds or a four-pound dumbbell? The dumbbell would, of course. The farther you move the mass from the point of rotation, the harder it is to twist it quickly. That's why target shooters add weight to their limb pockets — and why they shoot long bows — to get the mass as far away from their bow arm as possible for greater stability.

Now, let's look at the other type of torque–turning the bow from left to right. The cause may be as simple as the way you take your grip or the tension in your bow hand. Most bowhunters never realize they're torquing their bow. I always look to see if the bow is jumping straight forward when I shoot it. If it attempts to turn at all just as the arrow is leaving, I know my grip is whacked and I'm torquing the bow. The bow should be looking at the target until the arrow arrives.

Other than learning to shoot with a softer, more relaxed bow hand, the only

How To Shoot A Short Bow

Jim Hole, an outfitter in Alberta, Canada and a self-professed minimalist, uses a large clip to attach his 29-inch bow to his belt while climbing into his treestand just so he can eliminate the pull-up rope from his gear list. When you wear heavy clothing like Jim does, the sharper string angle of the short bow also helps keep the string away from his clothing and from his binoculars and calls while shooting. So, there are some practical reasons for carrying them. If you own or are planning to own a short bow, a little attention to shooting form will help you shoot it better.

Short bows are great in a ground blind and in a treestand where you may not have much room to maneuver. However, shooting these shorter bows takes a little practice and attention to shooting form.

The grip: If you've ever shot a slingshot you know that your pressure point on the grip is critical to consistency. Your hand position has to be perfect every time. Being off by even a small amount will throw your rock wide of the mark. The same is true of short bows. Because they don't have extended lever arms for stability like a longer bow, your grip becomes more critical. Your pressure point, the primary point of force between the bow and your hand, has to be identical on every shot. Pay particular attention to this aspect of your pre-shot routine and you'll become more consistent with your short bow.

If you are walking across Niagara Falls on a tight rope and are allowed to select a balancing pole, which do you want: a 40-foot pole that weighs 20 pounds or a four-foot pole that weighs 17 pounds? Obviously, the longer pole will increase stability, so if you opt for the shorter pole you need to be more careful. The same goes for shooting a short bow. You must be more conscious of keeping your bow hand perfectly relaxed throughout the shot.

Bow design: Conventional archery wisdom suggests that a bow with a high brace height is more forgiving than one with a low brace height. Since short bows are already somewhat less forgiving than long bows, it makes little sense to own one that also has a very low brace height. In this case, two negatives won't make a positive. A brace height over seven inches is a good basic setup when hunting with a short bow.

other way to combat this kind of shooting mistake is with a long stabilizer. Target shooters use long stabilizers because they produce maximum stability. Day in and day out, they can post better scores with a 36-inch stabilizer than with an eight-inch hunting model.

Of course, it is impractical to use a long stabilizer when hunting, even though it is more accurate. However, you should still take stability seriously, or at least consider it when buying a new bow or upgrading your old bow.

BOW WEIGHT AND STABILITY

The heavier the bow (regardless of length), the harder it is to move it quickly. That would suggest that a lightweight bow is less stable than a heavyweight bow. Most short bows are also very light, adding more support to the conclusion that shorter is not better.

THE EFFECTS ON ACCURACY

OK, that's enough physics nightmares. Bottom line: does the short bow make you less accurate? I believe that it does (or at least can). My reasoning is simple enough. As I already explained, the bow's length does resist rotation around one axis, so it has to be of some benefit. And a long bow weighs more, again increasing stability. If you look up and down the line at a big indoor target shoot, you're not going to find a 32-inch bow. More than likely everything will be over 40 inches. If length didn't matter, you'd see more short bows on the target line simply because there are more short bows on the market.

As mentioned, weight also has a very noticeable effect on accuracy. Several years back I shot what I'm sure was the heaviest bow I've ever owned. The bow was 43.5 inches long and weighed nearly six pounds without accessories. I shot that bow very well. It was like a rock at full draw. Its length and weight combined to make it extremely solid. I could feel the difference in the bow's stability while aiming and all the way through the shot. The bow just didn't wiggle around as much as lighter bows I'd shot. Purely from a weight standpoint, longer bows are more stable than shorter bows.

THIS IS HUNTING NOT TARGET SHOOTING

We need to put everything into perspective and look at this debate wearing our camo suits. How a bow works in the field is the real focus of this book. The

When belly crawling or shooting in tight locations, a short bow is a definite advantage.

average shot while hunting is not much past 20 yards. You don't really need Olympic-caliber shooting form to make clean kills at 20 yards, nor does your bow need to be the most stable or forgiving on the market. For archers of average shooting ability, the most important factor determining their success is steady nerves and good timing. These attributes are more important on most shots in the field than Olympic-caliber accuracy.

Yet I still like longer bows. Why? Because I shoot farther than 20 yards all the time. In fact, I want to drive tacks at 40 yards — that is my goal. So, there are in fact two categories of bowhunters: those who take only short shots and those who shoot farther.

If most of your shooting is at longer ranges or in competition, you will likely see an improvement in your accuracy when you switch to a longer bow. If your shooting form is good, the difference may be small. However, if you're prone to grab the grip or fight target panic at the point of release, you are likely to notice a greater difference.

THE UPSIDE TO BEING SHORT

There's more to this debate than just splitting hairs, literally and figuratively. There are hunting situations in which it is truly a pleasure to carry a short, lightweight bow. If you're hunting on foot for hours at a time, saving a pound or two can make the hunt more enjoyable. A short bow is also much easier to slide through the brush when you're crawling on the final approach of a long stalk. There is no arguing these advantages. But what about treestand hunting?

Your grip is extremely important when shooting a short bow because small changes in grip pressure have a greater influence on accuracy when the bow is short.

You don't need a 31- or 32-inch bow to get a shot at a buck from a tree. That is why they make limb saws so you can cut shooting lanes. For example, remember that lanky bow I wrote about earlier? The last four arrows that came out of Ol' Stretch before I retired him went into nice bucks — seriously. They were three whitetails and a mule deer right at the end of the season. All four bucks were taken from treestands. Did the 43.5-inch bow make the job harder? If it did, I sure didn't notice.

WRAP UP

If you have good shooting form, a short, lightweight bow is not going to have a noticeable effect on your ability to take game at common bowhunting distances of 20 to 25 yards. If the short, light bow increases your enjoyment, go for it. At the same time, a longer, heavier bow is not likely to make your hunting experience intolerable.

The average bowhunter won't notice much difference. This debate is really for the hunter who intends to take longer shots (such as 40-yard shots) or who competes in 3-D tournaments with his hunting bow. In this case, you'll find that a longer, heavier bow will help you shoot more consistently — even with good form. Yes, they are easier to carry, and I know everyone is buying them, but why do you want a short bow? If you don't really know, then there's no compelling reason to own one.

LOOKING AHEAD

Regardless of whether you shoot a long bow or a short bow, you still need to use good shooting form. Since your bow hand has more control over the bow than any other aspect of the shot, it is only logical that the bow's grip is a critical component of an accurate system. In the next chapter I'll get into the subject of selecting a bow based on how its grip feels. You may be surprised that this overlooked part of bow selection is actually one of the most important steps.

Chapter 11

GRIPS AND BOW TORQUE

The accumulation of little things is all that separates the great participants of any sport from the average ones. In archery, the important little things are not so obvious. You can get this knowledge only from years of practice, training and experience. Fortunately, archery has been around for a long time. You don't have to reinvent the wheel. The "little things" in archery are well understood and you can learn them the easy way, by talking to veterans and accomplished shooters.

The seemingly insignificant act of placing your hand on the bow is an example of one of these "little things" that are so critical to reaching your potential as a bowhunter. I am going to touch on shooting form just a little bit here so that you have the correct framework when deciding which bow has the best grip design for you.

SHOOTING FORM

If you shoot with a release aid, your bow hand is the only part of your body that actually touches the bow. It is the central point of control and feedback during the shot. Most archers never consider their grip, but it should be just the opposite. They should give more attention to their bow hand than almost any other aspect of shooting form.

A proper grip starts with a relaxed

The key to a great grip is a relaxed hand. How you take your grip will affect how well you shoot a bow.

hand. You'll never shoot to your ability if your bow hand is tense. This tension will creep into your aiming and it will become very difficult to make a natural follow through without trying to "help" the arrow. The bow will do just fine by itself; you don't have to help it.

Focus on your bow hand as you aim. Think of it as nothing more than a lifeless cradle at the end of your bow arm. It should do nothing (be completely dead) before, during and after the shot. Let your fingers hang naturally. Trying to force your hand to stay open will only increase tension.

CONSISTENT HAND POSITION

How you place your hand on the grip is just as important as keeping the hand relaxed. You can introduce torque by inconsistent hand placement. You definitely don't want to feel even the slightest bit of stretching in the skin of your hand. The very best hand placement allows you to apply the greatest force between the bow and your hand to a point directly in line with your forearm. This eliminates hinging of the wrist. You can find this point easily by pushing on the point where the lifelines of your palm come together. That is very close to the ideal pressure point.

Eventually, you won't have to look at your bow hand to know that you're lined up properly — you'll be able to instantly feel any small change in hand position. Raising your level of awareness regarding your bow hand is important in developing this sense. This is also where getting used to a specific bow has its advantages.

After you place your hand carefully on the grip, don't change the position of either your hand or your wrist until after the arrow is in the target. I see many archers bow their wrists and even slide their hands around on the grip as they draw the bow. This may put them in a more powerful position for drawing the bow, but it does great damage to consistent shooting. You'll never be consistent if you move your hand or wrist at any point after you initially settle it into position. Once your hand and wrist are set in place, leave them alone.

The quality of your grip starts before you draw the bow, determined first by your hand position.

GRIP DESIGN

You'll shoot most accurately when you reduce the total area of contact between your bow's grip and your hand. A wide grip, for example, gives you plenty of leverage for turning the bow. The handle will turn just as much as your hand turns. Conversely, when you use a narrow grip, contact more closely resembles a single point or a line. Now as you turn your hand, the bow doesn't react as much. You will notice a difference.

Some people like a wide grip because it feels more natural in their hand. If you will simply give a narrow grip a chance, you soon become used to the feel and it will soon be natural enough. A narrow grip is important. I have tested hundreds of bows over the years and a grip with a throat measuring one-inch, or less, (down to three-quarter inch) feels and shoots best for me.

A grip's design can affect accuracy in other ways, as well. I've owned bows that were difficult to tune and shoot accurately. It always came down to the way the grip felt in my hand. I could tune these bows, but only when I gripped them in a very uncomfortable manner. Generally, the biggest problem with these grips was their shape, not their width. Through the narrowest point, these grips were definitely narrow enough, but the lower portion of the grip was wider or it was set at an angle that was far from accommodating my normal hand position.

This brings up another point. The comfort of the grip is another very important aspect to consider when choosing a bow. When it comes down to selecting between two different bows that both fit you, always pick the one that feels the best in your hand. With a comfortable grip, you'll be able to relax your hand and shoot properly.

You may run into the terms low wrist, mid wrist and high wrist. These are all grip styles. They describe the angle of the grip. A low wrist grip is very flat, nearly vertical on the bow. A high wrist grip is much more angled so your wrist has to tip up higher so your hand will fit. Most people will do best with a low wrist grip so they can use the recommended pressure point (approximately where their lifelines come together) with ease.

A thin grip such as PSE's B.E.S.T. grip design offers less contact and applies pressure in one area or line making hand torque more difficult to apply.

However, if you simply can't get comfortable gripping a bow with a low wrist, the mid wrist is the second best choice. I don't recommend the high wrist grip because it becomes too difficult to apply the correct pressure point to the grip. You end up feeling like you don't have any strength when drawing the bow.

Self-grip: Many excellent archers simply do away with the grip altogether. They remove it from the bow and shoot the bow right off the back of the riser. This ensures that their line of contact and pressure point will be as narrow as possible and typically allows the lowest possible wrist position. Some bows will accommodate this better than others. Some have a riser section that

When choosing a bow, the comfort of the grip should be a big influence on your decision. Always pick the bow that feels best in your hand.

is too sharp-edged in this area to permit the self-grip. Of course there is always the metal file, but before you start rounding off your riser, call the warranty department of the bow company in question and get their advice. Without question they have dealt with this request in the past and can give you guidelines that ensure your safety and keep your warranty intact.

After removing the grip, you have a few choices. You can either shoot it right off the metal or you can wrap something around the grip section. Some archers use a small piece of leather and then either duct tape it in place or use black electrical tape to hold it securely around the grip area. This serves to increase your insulation on cold days (a bow's riser can be very, very cold on a cold day) and it smoothes out any sharp edges. You can also simply apply the tape without the thin piece of leather to improve the feel of the grip.

Tacky versus slippery: I have seen many soft rubber grips through the years and there are still a few on the market. I don't like them for one very important reason — they are too tacky. When placing your hand on the grip, it is impossible to slide it easily into the lowest torque position with a soft rubber grip. The grip grabs your hand or glove before your hand is settled. Not only is this annoying and uncomfortable, it actually will increase the likelihood that you will apply torque to the bow during the shot. If you have a favorite bow but it has a soft rubber grip, consider taking it off and shooting the bow without a grip as described in the last section. The ideal grip is one that is slippery so your hand can easily find its natural low torque position.

Don't forget the grip. By spending just as much time considering your grip as you do considering your arrow speed, you can take the steps needed to eliminate torque and improve accuracy in the field.

LOOKING AHEAD

We are pretty close to wrapping up the discussion on the ideal hunting bow. I hope you have a good idea what makes for an accurate bow in the field. Now it is time to find one that is affordable. I love finding deals, and I'm sure you do too. It is part of being a member of a capitalistic society. Of course, a good deal means not only a cheap price, but also a solid value. The goods still need to be there. In the next chapter I'll help you find value in today's marketplace.

Chapter 12

BUYING BOWS ON A BUDGET

W hile it is sure fun to look at all the brand new bows that hit the market each year, reality eventually sets in when we take that much-dreaded peek at the price tag and then into our billfolds. The gap is as wide as the Grand Canyon. Might as well be trying out for the Yankees or facing Tiger Woods in the U.S. Open, or Roger Federer at Wimbledon. It is the same feeling we have on April 15 each year when we sign our income tax return.

When reality sets in, we start to look at the rest of the bows in each company's catalog — those on the third and fourth page. In this chapter, I hope to help you make sense of this market and find the best bows for the money. Value is the goal — good performance at a good price.

It is realistic to find a good bow for under $400. While the top name bows are often much higher, you don't need the most expensive bow to fill a freezer with venison or wapiti flanks. A sub-$400 bow is the goal. I'll get into affordable accessories in a future chapter; here I am going to stay focused on the bows.

In the process of summarizing several of the best values, I'll offer a few tips on what to look for when buying a used bow — another great way to get the most bang for the buck. Given the heavy use of auction sites on the Internet, like eBay, it is easy to find a good used bow — if you know what you are looking for. Some of these bows are just as good as their brand new, higher priced brothers. Why pay more if you aren't getting more?

ARROW SPEED

Some manufacturers segment their bows into price ranges based on arrow speed. They keep their fastest and latest cam designs and cutting edge features exclusively for their most expensive bows.

A little perspective is in order. Today, most of the economical bows are as fast as the speed burners of a decade ago. They will produce IBO speeds of approximately 300 to 310 fps. When matched with the right arrow, that is fast enough for any kind of bowhunting. So, don't get hung up on speed beyond a reasonable minimum. Yes, fast bows are fun to shoot and they will improve your success rate slightly over the long run, but they are generally considerably more expensive. Solid performance is all you need. A good goal is a bow with an IBO speed of at least 300 fps.

RISER CONSTRUCTION IS LEAST IMPORTANT

When looking for value, I would not sacrifice too much arrow speed. As mentioned in the last section, you can have solid performance at a good price. Instead, I would plan to give up a few fancy, unnecessary frills. For example, you don't need a finely machined riser to shoot a dump truck load of game over your lifetime. A cast or extruded riser with little or no machine work is just as effective at holding the limbs and accessories in place, but it is much less expensive to manufacture. For that reason, bows with no bells and whistles tend to be more affordable.

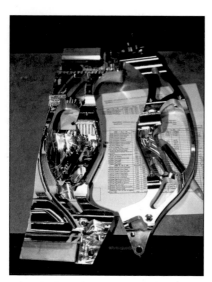

Some risers require a lot of machine time to make and this is reflected in the price. However, you don't need an intricately machined riser to shoot game.

Here is an example. Looking in one company's line, you can have their flagship model with a price tag of $599.95 with a fully machined riser or you can have one of their lower end bows with a much less frilly riser at $329.95. Both have single cams, parallel limbs and IBO speeds of 300 fps. I'm not going to tell you what to do, but I know which one I would buy. They both have the same warranty; the cheaper riser is not going to bust. Hmmm, what to do?

I also looked in a different manufacturer's line. There I found another classic example of an economical riser bringing the price of a bow down from the stratosphere. They built the low-end bow around an extruded riser with a limited amount of machine work. While the company's top of the line bows sell for nearly $800, this model has a suggested retail price of $399. With an IBO speed of 304 fps, it is fast enough, is portable and forgiving. It is all you need.

The list of economical bows that will shoot just as many animals as their more expensive counterparts is long. The goal is to find the very best value. Generally, the best value is not the flagship bow. The goal of these bows is to skim off the top dollar from people who always want the very newest and best. True value lies not on the first page of the catalog but on the fourth or fifth page.

WHERE NOT TO SKIMP

I've already said I would skimp on the riser before anything else. However, there are some things I am not willing to give up for the sake of a few dollars. First off, I would make sure the bow had a great grip. I got way into this subject in the last chapter. If the grip is not good and you aren't comfortable shooting the bow with the grip removed, don't buy it. Surely, there are other bows that will work better. One of the very best value bows I have ever tested was ruined by a blocky, square grip. It did everything perfectly, but it felt terrible. I couldn't recommend it. It is not worth the savings to own a bow with a nasty grip.

I would also make certain the bow has a good string. It is really hard to tell how good the string is without owning the bow and shooting it for a few months, but there are two telltale signs that will help you avoid buying a bow with a cheap string. First, look at the cam or cams. If they are over-rotated (turned farther around than they should be), it is obvious the string has already stretched from the time they built the bow. That tells me the company used a cheap string that will likely keep stretching for many months to come.

Of course, this presumes that you know where the cam is supposed to be when correctly set up. It is worth finding out by asking the customer service person before you buy the bow, or even the archery shop pro if he or she seems experienced and trustworthy.

Second, look at the string's center serving. If the serving appears at all loose, or you can move the top few rounds with your thumbnail, it is a cheap

A high quality string and harness are critical. Don't skimp in this area.

string. If it has monofilament center serving, forget it.

Cheap strings are my pet peeve. They stretch, the serving separates or breaks and everything changes from one week to the next. Bowhunting is tough enough without having to deal with a string that is changing.

I would never skimp on arrow flight. Don't accept poor arrow flight just because the bow is cheap. Affordable bows can shoot perfect arrows just as well as expensive bows. There are plenty of them that do and it is not worth fighting a bow that you can't tune. Shoot the bow before you buy it. Ask to tune the bow. If it won't tune, try a different one. Don't buy it regardless of price. Even a free bow that produces bad arrow flight is a liability, not an asset.

I don't want a loud bow either, nor one that bucks violently in my hand when

If your bow tunes and shoots a straight arrow accurately and with sufficient speed to counteract slight errors in range estimation, that is all you need – regardless of price.

I shoot it. The days of loud, hard recoiling bows are over. Even affordable bows are now very tame in the hand and easy on the ears. If the one you are considering isn't, keep looking. Plenty of other brands will be, at a good price.

BUYING A USED BOW

Many of my friends upgrade to a new bow every two or three years whether they need one or not. Most times, they really don't need one, but they like new bows. They either give their old bow away to a new bowhunter who can't afford one or they sell it. Most archery shops won't mess with used bows, but you can find them by the dozens on the auction website, www.ebay.com. Here's what you need to know so you don't get the shaft when buying a used bow.

Stick with proven bows from name brand manufacturers that are still in business. That way you can get service and parts if needed. Because you are buying used, you can afford to buy one of the top of the line bows, and that should produce some level of confidence that it is a quality tool. I would expect to pay roughly two-thirds of current retail for a very popular, top-name bow that is just one year-old and in lightly used condition.

As they get older, you should expect to pay less. To be honest, the best values are in bows that have been out of the limelight for a year or two. You should be able to get some very good bows for around $350. You can get some nice, fully loaded bows (with all the accessories you need) for under $500.

Now for the tricky part, how do you know you are not buying someone else's lemon? By sticking with name brand bows, you have some assurance in that regard. Also, some sellers will take returns if the bow doesn't meet your satisfaction. You can look at the feedback scores for the seller

When looking over a used bow be sure to check the center serving. If the serving material isn't in great shape, you'll need to seriously consider replacing it immediately.

posted with his or her listing to get some idea how reputable the seller is and how much you can trust the seller to describe their offering accurately. After that, it comes down to the old saying, "let the buyer beware." For insurance, I would only buy a bow that comes with a trial and return guarantee.

If you are buying a used bow from a friend or acquaintance and have the opportunity to inspect it first, shoot a few arrows out of it. Try paper tuning the bow (shooting arrows through paper at a range of six feet to judge whether the arrows are making nice, clean bullet holes). If you can't get it to tune, forget it. There are definitely a few bad apples out there. Not all bows shoot well.

When purchasing a used bow, stick with brand names/models and companies that are still in business. This will allow you to get parts when they are needed.

If you don't have the opportunity to shoot the bow first, examine the cams to make sure they are lined up with the string. Sight down the string and compare it to the two cams or to the cam and idler (if it is a single-cam bow). If they aren't lined up, it is likely that the string will travel sideways slightly when you release it and the arrow will fishtail from side to side. Look for a different bow.

Most problems with a bow revolve around the limbs. When studying a used bow, spend plenty of time on the limbs. Look for any signs of cracks (even little hairline cracks). Also, look at the string and harnesses for signs of wear. Strings and harnesses aren't cheap, so if you have to replace them right away, the bow may not be such a bargain.

If you are new to bowhunting or looking for an upgrade from Uncle Bob's hand-me-down, don't despair; you don't have to spend a fortune to get a great, high quality hunting bow.

Kit Bows: A Viable Alternative

When buying new, kit bows are generally the most inexpensive way to put together a solid, functional bow rig. There is a stigma surrounding kit bows that they are "cheap" or insufficient for most bowhunters needs. This misconception couldn't be

Kit bows are another good way to extend your buying power because they generally permit you to save money on all neccessary accessories.

further from the truth (in most modern cases). Several companies have specialized in value-oriented kit bows. I've seen some very functional rigs that sell for as little as $440, complete with everything you need except a release aid and broadheads. If you are a relatively new bowhunter looking to set up a bow starting from scratch, make sure to check out the kit bows before you start handing out a bunch of Benjamin Franklins for the latest and greatest.

LOOKING AHEAD

That's it for bows. Next, I'm going to get into the accessories that you need to make the bow shoot accurately; rests, sights, releases, slings, quivers, etc. If you thought there were too many options to consider when selecting your bow, you had better take a deep breath and sit down, because you can fill a catalog with all the accessory choices. Fortunately, I have tried most of them and can help you separate the foam from the fluid. Accessories will become much easier to understand once we wade through the tradeoffs. You will soon know enough to buy just what you need to make your bow complement your style of hunting perfectly.

Chapter 13

SIGHT OPTIONS

You have to decide what style to buy, how many pins you need, what type of pins to use and how to set them. In this chapter, it is my goal to lay out the options and discuss the trade-offs. I want you to make a good decision, because your sight is the only thing that will appear between your eye and your quarry. Sights are important.

FIXED-PIN SIGHTS

Fixed-pin sights are by far the most common style used by bowhunters. An example is a simple three-pin sight. The bowhunter may then set the pins for 20, 30 and 40 yards. Fixed-pin sights give you simplicity but don't necessarily deliver ultimate precision. Assume you have set your pins for 20, 30 and 40 yards and the animal is standing at 36 yards. You will have to hold your 30-yard pin high or your 40-yard pin low. You will probably opt for holding the 30-yard pin high. How high? Good question.

A fixed, three-pin design is perfect for most whitetail hunters. However, out West and in wide open locales, archers require more pins where shot distance on average is longer, requiring individually sighted in pins for downrange accuracy.

Unless you have practiced a lot at these intermediate distances, you have introduced doubt at a time when what you really need is commitment. This is not a huge deal if you are shooting a fast bow, because the flat trajectory will compensate for some errors in judgment on your part. However, if you are shooting a slower arrow (under 260 fps) or the shot is not as close (suppose it is 43 yards), there remains some question about where to aim.

Fixed-pin sights have strengths too. They are simple. You don't have to do anything before

For three years, I hunted with just two pins, a 20-yard pin and a 40-yard pin. I never shot past 40 yards and I gapped between them for 30-yard shots. That system was simple but it wasn't truly accurate. You want to use the least number of pins possible to keep things simple so you don't accidentally choose the wrong one during the excitement, but you want to make sure your gaps are never wider than 10 yards. Ideally, I should have been shooting a three-pin sight.

Using this system, you merely need to know your maximum range and you can quickly decide how many pins to use. For example, if you will not shoot past 30 yards, you can get by with two pins — you might even be able to make it work with just one pin if your bow is fast enough. If your maximum range is 60 yards, you will likely be most accurate with five pins.

you draw and shoot. With some practice, you can learn to hold high or low by the required amount to be accurate at all distances. Most bowhunters will do well with a simple three-pin sight. They are affordable, and they work great for the majority of hunting situations.

MOVEABLE PIN SIGHTS

When using a moveable pin sight, you have to adjust it for the distance of the shot. There's a pointer and scale and some type of moving carriage that work together to permit you to quickly adjust the single pin to the exact distance of the shot. Think of it in these terms: you raise your rangefinder and discover that the animal is 33 yards away. Then you set the sight for 33 yards and aim dead-on with the pin. Nothing could be more precise or simpler.

When you know the exact distance of the shot and have time to move the pin, a moveable pin sight is most accurate because you can aim dead-on without any confusion about where to hold.

Moveable pin sights have their place in bowhunting; they are ideal when timing is not rushed and precision is critical. In other words, when you have the time to set the sight before drawing and shooting, they are awesome. And they are especially useful when the shots you take are long enough to require pinpoint aiming (not gapping between pins).

Nearly all archers are more accurate when they can aim dead-on with a single pin than when they have to figure the proper holdover. If it weren't so, the professional archers wouldn't be shooting moveable pin sights in the open class of 3-D tournaments. The only way you're going to have a pin for every possible yardage

The author prefers fixed pin sights that have a gang adjustable sight head.

is to use a sight that has a moveable pin. This is the most accurate possible system, but there is a glaring weakness. When the animal moves after you set the pin and draw the bow, you are back to guessing, but now without any other pins to offer a frame of reference.

I've shot a fair amount of game, and I've learned one valuable lesson: I'm not cool enough under fire to do a lot of intelligent, creative thinking. It's about all I can do to stick with my normal routine: estimate range, pick a pin and focus on the spot. If you throw in more steps and ask for greater judgment, I'm likely to do something really dumb — like shoot the arrow straight up in the air. For this reason, I've always rejected moveable pin sights. But, recent changes in the way some are constructed has changed my thinking.

There is a way that you can benefit from the advantages of a single moveable pin without giving up the flexibility of multiple pins. Several companies make moveable pin sights with compact sight bodies having three pins. With this system, you can set the sight to its closest setting and then, without moving it, sight in the three pins for 20, 30 and 40 yards. Until you move the slide, you have a three-pin fixed pin sight.

You can easily enjoy the benefits of a moveable pin sight by using the slide to sight in the top pin for a full range of shots. Now, you have a valuable option. You can adjust the top pin for exact distance of the shot or you can leave the sight alone and not move it to use it as three-pin, fixed-pin sight — the best of both worlds.

IMPORTANT FEATURES

Every sight, whether having a moveable pin or fixed pins, should feature bright fiber optics so you can see the aiming points well, even in low light. The brightest pins are those with long fibers that extend at least six inches. Some pins have fibers that extend as much as two to three feet and are wrapped a number of times inside of a spool or around the pin guard. I recommend these wrapped or spooled fiber pins; bright is good when facing a shot on an overcast day right at

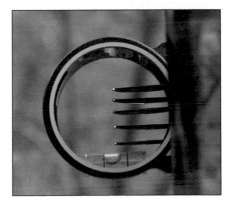

A fiber optic sight with bright, spooled fibers that are well protected is ideal for bowhunting.

Sight-In Techniques

Sight in your bow over the course of at least one week. That way you can average out your shooting form. If you try to set your sight pins during just one day of shooting, you run the risk that your shooting form will be off that day and you will set the pins to accommodate your flawed form. Get the pins close after the first session and then tweak them a little at a time over the next several sessions until you are hitting your aiming point every time.

If the bow is shooting high, you have to move your pins up. If the bow is shooting low, move them down. If the bow is shooting left, move them left and if the bow is shooting right, move them right.

You also need to understand that if you are canting (leaning) your bow when aiming, you will shoot to the side. If you are tipping the bow to the right, you will hit to the right. This is not ideal unless you can lean the bow exactly the same amount every time you shoot. The best strategy is to use a sight with a bubble level so you can remove this variable from your shooting. The bubble level will encourage you to hold the bow upright on every shot.

Sighting in a bow takes several days in order to get things perfect. Take your time and conscientiously sight in each sight pin.

the beginning or end of legal shooting time.

The size of the pin (the diameter of the fiber) is also a factor to consider. You can buy pins that range from .019-inch diameter up to .039-inch diameter. I am a firm believer that the larger diameter fibers are more visible in low light, so I like the .039-inch pins. However, at longer distances, the larger pin's head will block a greater portion of the target, prompting some archers to prefer the smaller pins. It is a personal choice, really. I have used the .039-inch pins out to 60 yards without any problems, but someone else might prefer a different sight picture. That is the fun of bowhunting; you can customize the gear to fit your individual taste.

If you are planning to use a fixed-pin sight, be sure to get one with a gang-adjustable sight head. There are very few models on the market that aren't gang-adjustable, but I thought I had better add this paragraph just to make sure you understand what you are buying. Gang-adjustable simply means that you can move the sight head up and down and side to side without moving the individual pins within the head. They remain locked in the head as you move it. Being gang-adjustable makes it much easier to sight-in the bow and easier to make changes later. Don't be tempted by a cheap price to buy a sight that doesn't have a gang-adjustable head. It will be a nightmare to sight-in and change later.

LOOKING AHEAD

Sights are important, but how you set them up and use them is also very important. In the next chapter, I will go into details on my favorite way to use sights and peeps. If you haven't tried this method, you are in for a pleasant surprise.

Chapter 14

BIG PEEPS AND ROUND PIN GUARDS

Y ou can change two pieces of gear during the off season that will improve your accuracy dramatically in the fall. First, use a sight with a round pin guard and second, use a huge peep sight to change the way you aim — for the better. You will benefit from a more consistent anchor point and improved visibility of the target without giving up any accuracy.

Several years ago, I posted a question on www.edersbow.com bowhunting website to test the knowledge of the site's visitors relative to their anchor point. More than 50 percent of the several hundred people who took the bait had no idea that their anchor point moved every time they changed their shot distance. If you use more than one pin (or use a moveable pin sight) and center the appropriate pin in your peep sight when aiming, your anchor point has to move up and down on your face. It does this in order for your peep sight to line up with each pin. Your anchor point drops for longer shots and rises for shorter shots. I, for one, never liked this.

Every bowhunter has one anchor point that feels better than any other. Suppose your anchor point feels best when you center your 30-yard pin; when you switch

With a large peep aperture and round pin guard, you can use your most comfortable anchor point on every shot, regardless of the distance.

to your 20-yard pin, you have to raise your anchor point to center that pin in the peep. Now go back to 40 yards and center that pin. Your anchor point will have to go down. Though it moves slightly, it does move.

The slower your arrow, the greater your pin gap and the more you will have to move your anchor point up and down to keep the various pins centered. The affects are also magnified for archers who set long-range pins for Western hunting. Unless you practice a lot at every distance, you are likely to feel uncomfortable changing your anchor point this often. There is another way (in my opinion, a better way) to aim that lets you keep the same anchor point for every shot.

Use a round pin guard and a large peep sight, and center the entire pin guard inside your peep sight when aiming, regardless of how many pins you use. Don't center the individual pins. This system has two primary benefits.

A round pin guard allows you to center the entire pin guard inside a large peep sight.

BENEFITS

Never change your anchor point: Every year more sight companies are putting round pin guards on their sights. Because the pin guard is round, you can easily center it in your peep sight for every shot and forget about centering the individual pins.

To shoot near or far, all you have to do is lower or raise the bow until the proper pin is on the spot; your anchor point remains the same (presumably in its most comfortable position). Because you are still centering the pin guard, you don't give up any precision or accuracy in the process.

The ability to use a larger peep: I missed a chip shot at a giant whitetail more than a decade ago. The shot still haunts me and still affects my equipment choices. I missed that buck because I couldn't see my pins well enough through the peep, even though it was still legal shooting time. I think of that lesson every time I set up a bow. Since then, I've switched to brighter pins, but I still had trouble seeing them right at the beginning and end of legal shooting time.

The pins were clearly visible when I looked around the peep but everything turned fuzzy and murky when I looked through it. I considered opening my peep up but then the pins seemed to swim in a wide expanse.

Granted, a minority (less than 20 per-

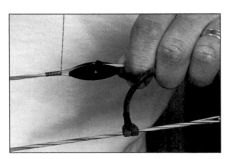

The size of the hole in your peep makes a big difference in your ability to see clearly in low light.

cent) of my shots at game have come during the first and last half-hour of legal shooting time, but among those have been a couple of the biggest bucks I've ever shot at. It makes sense to prepare just as well for low light shots as for those that occur in full light. In fact, it makes a lot of sense to spend at least 20 percent of your time practicing under low light conditions.

If you center a round pin guard inside a grossly oversized peep sight, you have the best of all worlds: great visibility and great accuracy. Being large, such peeps permit the maximum amount of light to reach your eye and they increase your field of view, but because you are centering the pin guard tightly inside its borders, you give up nothing in accuracy.

In typical cases, you are going to need a peep with a hole that's one-quarter inch in diameter. Several companies make peeps this large. Jump on the Internet; you will be able to find several quickly. I have even begun seeing peeps that exceed one-quarter inch in diameter.

Making the change: If you've spent years mastering the art of centering each pin in your peep before releasing the string, it will take at least two

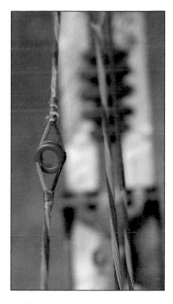

A large peep, such as the Meta one-quarter inch model from G5 Outdoors, allows plenty of light to reach your eye when aiming in low light.

months to retrain your instincts to begin centering the pin guard instead. I suggest that if you like the idea, you should begin practicing this style immediately.

Allow plenty of time on the range to get used to any new style of shooting a bow.

Given two months of practice, you should be centering the pin guard naturally.

If you head into the season still having to remind yourself to center the guard instead of the pin on every shot, you are setting yourself up for a miss. You had better start practicing with a vengeance or change back to centering the pin immediately. Under the pressure of a shot at game, you will fall back on your instincts. You must be sure to practice enough to assure the method you fall back on is the same one you used when sighting-in the bow.

LOOKING AHEAD

While we have covered fixed and moveable pin sights in detail, there is yet another style that many bowhunters use. I get more questions about pendulum sights than the other two styles combined. They solve certain problems when hunting from a treestand, so they have a place in the market. In the next chapter, I will go over the trade-offs so you can decide whether there should be a pendulum sight on your whitetail bow.

Chapter 15

UNDERSTANDING PENDULUM SIGHTS

After a few years of practice with a bow, hitting a pie plate every time at 30 yards is not particularly challenging — knowing the range is the key to accuracy for accomplished archers. You can be the best shot in the world, but if you misjudge a 30-yard shot by five yards, you won't hit where you are aiming. Anything you can do to improve your accuracy at unknown distances will increase the amount of meat in your freezer.

If you hunt primarily out of treestands and your shots are typically 30 yards or less, and you have no desire to shoot farther, pendulums might be the pefect sight for your hunting setup.

Though it's possible when stand hunting to use a laser rangefinder to pre-measure the distances to various landmarks, all too often deer will approach from a direction you didn't expect. Or, they may come in too fast or on a course that's too unpredictable to permit you to range the animal directly and still be at full draw at the right moment.

As I look back over the last several years, I've shot a lot of deer from a treestand — counting the does. Of those I shot at past 20 yards, I was able to use the rangefinder on about half. Overall, I figured I knew the range almost exactly on about 75 percent of the deer I have shot. That means that although a good, fast laser rangefinder hung around my neck, I still had to judge the distance by eye on some of them. Range estimation will always play an important role in treestand hunting.

Wouldn't it be nice if you could use a single pin and hold it dead-on, regardless of the distance of the shot? It would sure remove a lot of guesswork. There are only two ways to achieve this goal: shoot a super fast arrow (approximating a bullet from a gun) or use a pendulum bow sight (for shots out to about 35 yards). Pendulums offer the treestand hunter accuracy and simplicity.

HOW PENDULUM SIGHTS WORK

Pendulum sights have a primary pin that is free to pivot. In most cases, the pin is in a secondary sight body that pivots within the primary sight body. This secondary sight body hangs straight down, regardless of bow angle. Gravity holds it in this position.

As the angle of shot changes, the pin never rotates relative to the ground, only relative to the sight body. For example, suppose you point the bow downward for a close-range shot. The pin swings as the bow angle changes (the pin pivots within the sight). As a result, the aiming point appears much higher within the sight window — which is what you need for a close shot. It occupies the same position as a very short-range pin.

If you raise the bow for a longer shot, the pin again pivots within the sight body. Now the aiming point appears much lower in the sight window. In this position, it will act just like a long-range pin. One pin does it all — automatically. The angle of the bow at various distances causes the pin to adjust for the shot.

You have to sight in your pendulum sight from the same height from which you plan to hunt. After that, it will automatically compensate for all shot distances from five yards out to roughly 30 yards.

THE DOWNSIDE OF PENDULUM SIGHTS

All pendulums have a range limit at which their compensation ability begins to break down. Most advertise that they are good out to a range of approximately 30 yards. After that, you'll begin to shoot low. If you shoot a fast arrow (more than

Pendulum sights work off the angle of the bow to automatically compensate for shot range.

approximately 265 fps) this maximum distance may be closer to 32 or 33 yards.

Pendulum sights also lose a portion of their effectiveness on uphill and downhill shots. Because these sights gain their range compensation ability from the angle of the bow, not the actual distance, slopes can fool them because the bow angle changes but the distance doesn't.

In general, you'll find yourself shooting low on downhill shots and high on uphill shots. Moderate downhill shots present little problem. However, shots to an upslope (even though you may still be aiming downward) and sharply downhill shots are a problem with a pendulum. For such shots, use a ground-level pin (most pendulum sights allow the installation of at least one stationary pin) instead of the swinging pendulum.

As a general guideline, if you will be hunting a lot on sidehills, where the elevation changes from one side of your stand to the other, pendulum sights are too easily fooled and are not the best choice for you.

Practice from stand height in order to be sure your pendulum sight is properly sighted-in. Typically, pendulums max out on accuracy at about 30 yards.

Changes in treestand height affect accuracy in the same way as shots on steep slopes. Sight-in from your average treestand height. In other words, if you typically hunt between 16 and 20 feet off the ground, sight in from a stand that is 18 feet high. If your stands vary in height by more than a few feet, you'll notice a slight loss in accuracy. In general, you'll tend to hit slightly low if you go several feet above your sight-in height and slightly high if you drop down several feet. Test your shooting from various stand heights before you begin hunting.

Of course, pendulum sights also offer a disadvantage if you also plan to use the same sight when hunting from the ground. Some pendulums give you the option of locking the pivot in place and then adjusting the entire sight head for various ground level shot distances. However, most pendulum sights are dedicated treestand only systems.

HOW TO PICK A PENDULUM SIGHT

Quiet operation: Pendulum sights have moving parts and thus have the potential to be noisy if the parts don't fit snugly together. Most of the pendulum sights made by the name brand sight companies have smooth bearings and are acceptably quiet. They use well-designed bushings or even snug ball bearings to retain the swinging pin. If you can, shoot the sight you are interested in before you buy it to see if it is noisy.

Fiber optics: Not all pendulum sights have fiber optic pins. When attempting to upgrade your sight, there's no reason to take one step forward and another step backward. Choose only the pendulums that offer excellent pin visibility. This usually translates into lighted pins or fiber optic pins.

Shown is an example of a pendulum sight. The sight pin swings to stay vertical as the bow angle changes, automatically compensating for shot distance.

Arrow speed adjustments: Today's bows are so fast that even pendulum sights that aren't adjustable for arrow speed will perform well. However, if you want to wring the most possible accuracy out of your pendulum sight, check out those that you can adjust to match your arrow speed.

I don't use pendulum sights even though I hunt from treestands most of the time. I don't have a big problem with range estimation errors because I shoot a fast arrow. I hunt bluff country a lot and the ground is rarely level. I also shoot past 30 yards routinely and don't want to bother with the swinging pin.

However, pendulum sights offer a real advantage to the treestand hunter who hunts primarily from trees growing on level, or near-level, ground. They eliminate the need to worry about shot distance out to 30 yards. If you are a good shot but have trouble estimating distance well and choosing the right pin during the excitement of encounters with game, nothing beats the simplicity of a pendulum sight. Just pull up, plant the pin and release the string.

LOOKING AHEAD

We've covered sights, and now it is time to move on to the next important accessory item for your bow: the arrow rest. When you consider the parts of the bow that touch your arrow, they are precious few, only the string and the rest. I've already gone into detail on how to choose a quality string. Now it is time to get into the subject of arrow rests. If the rest isn't good, the shot won't be good either. Read on and you will find out how to choose the perfect rest.

REST
OPTIONS

During the three decades that separate me from my first years in archery, the industry has seen some incredible changes, starting with the development of the first spring-loaded, two-prong arrow rest in the '70s. That's when Freddie Troncoso at Golden Key Futura began selling the TM Hunter — one of history's most popular hunting rests. That single invention did more to revolutionize arrow rests than anything that came along in the next 20 years. However, in the past several years a new wave of change threatens to make these old school arrow rests obsolete.

Full capture rests such as the popular Whisker Biscuit hold the arrow snugly in place. During the shot, there is no effort made to eliminate fletching contact with the rest, but rather it is balanced on all three fletchings at the same time to keep good arrow flight.

Arrow rest makers now realize that if they are serious about selling rests to bowhunters, their products must prevent any possibility that the arrow might fall off the rest. Second, they must permit excellent arrow flight with small diameter carbon arrows. Today's rests are better than anything I have seen in three decades. If you are getting into archery now, you are getting in at the right time. It has never been easier to shoot a straight flying arrow.

Of course, conventional arrow rests, similar to Fred Troncoso's original TM Hunter, are still around, but the tide is going out. Here are the new rests that are shaping the future and providing perfect arrow flight for today's bowhunters. I recommend these rest styles for trouble free bowhunting.

CAPTURE RESTS

The ultimate hunting rest should cradle the arrow securely so it won't bounce free when the string is drawn or when the wind blows hard. It should even go so far as to keep the arrow on the rest when the bow is carried through the brush during the last 40 yards of a stalk or when you lay it across your lap while sitting on stand. It should promote good arrow flight and be rugged enough to handle several long, tough seasons. Finally, the perfect hunting arrow rest should have as few pieces as possible (and ideally no moving parts) so it will be entirely dependable and extremely quiet.

New Archery Products' full capture, NAP 360° Capture Rest uses one set of brushes and a Teflon post to hold the arrow in place.

Full capture rests take a number of forms. Some have three launchers pointing inward toward the shaft. Others, like the Whisker Biscuit, which started this trend, have a hole in the middle of an inward pointing circle of bristles. Most capture rests fall into one of these two standard styles.

In one of my recurring nightmares, I draw my bow, aim at a big buck and then watch as the arrow veers sickeningly wide of the animal. The cause of the horrible miss is quickly determined. The arrow fell off the rest before I drew the bow. Thankfully, that nightmare has not played out for real, and it probably never will. While I've always made every effort to be sure my arrow is resting properly before I drew, I recently switched to a rest that eliminates this problem from ever occurring.

Though I've escaped unscathed, my nightmare has been reality for many bowhunters with whom I've spoken. I even shared an elk camp with a guy that missed a very good bull because his arrow slipped off the rest during the final stages of the encounter. And this guy wasn't a rookie either. Properly set up, full capture rests will keep the arrow on the rest and ready for action no matter what. That's the main reason bowhunters have been, and will continue to be, interested in this style of rest.

There is, however, a second reason capture rests are a good choice for bowhunters. Because the rest contacts the shaft on all sides, it is better able to guide the arrow and soak up the arrow flight discrepancies caused by imperfect nock travel. Recently, a friend of mine has been calling with experiences he and his shooting buddy are having with one of these models. It seems that every bow they set up produced a perfect bullet hole through paper right from the very first arrow, regardless of whether they used aluminum or carbon shafts.

I tried one on my own hunting bow. I wanted to see if I could find any differences compared to the drop-away rest I'd been using. After tweaking the rest until the arrows hit in the same place, I noticed no difference in arrow flight or accuracy. The bow shot just as well at 50 yards with the capture rest as it had with the drop-away rest. Also, I think the bow may have shot just a bit quieter due to the fact that the rest has no moving parts.

Full capture rests make no pretense about eliminating fletching contact. In fact, they guarantee contact. But, because of the way the rest is designed, the contact doesn't throw the arrow off course. Instead, this full contact serves to soak up extraneous movement in the arrow and actually smoothes out the flight.

The process of squeezing an arrow out of one these rests is kind of like pressing Play-Doh through one of those little extruders that permit children to make star-shaped dough logs. The shaft has little choice but to come out straight.

The 360-degree bristles of the Whisker Biscuit, for example, illustrate another advantage of capture rests: there is no wrong way to load the arrow. As long as one of the vanes doesn't hit the cables, the rest will produce good arrow flight regardless of where the fletchings are pointing.

Full capture rests have only one true negative. Some will beat the bejiminy out of your fletchings. Because of the amount of contact that occurs during the shot, long helical fletchings are especially vulnerable. However, by using a stiff, short fletching (there are several on the market now, typified by the Bohning Blazer) you can reduce damage to an acceptable level.

DROP-AWAY RESTS

Drop-away arrow rests fall during the shot to clear out of the way of the arrow's fletching. The ideal sequence has the rest supporting and stabilizing the forward travel of the arrow for as long as possible before dropping away just in time to miss the fletchings. Fletching contact with the rest is the number one cause of poor arrow flight with conventional arrow rests, but these drop-away rests solve that problem.

Drop-away rests are the best choice for bowhunters using carbon arrows with long fletching and a high degree of helical offset. It can be

Short, stiff fletchings such as Bohning's Blazer work best with full capture rests because they are not as easily wrinkled as they pass through.

Shown is an example of a typical drop-away rest; Cobra Archery's Double Diamond.

tough to tune these small diameter arrows with conventional rests because the launchers need to be set so close together to hold the shaft that they create interference with the fletching. And these long fletchings can become tattered quickly with popular capture rests.

Though not as critical, aluminum arrow users will also find that drop-away rests can solve tough fletching contact problems. I've shot various styles of drop away rests for seven years and have found them to be reliable and easy to tune with a well-made bow.

One of the great advantages of drop-away rests is their ability to hold an arrow solidly in place until you release the string. Because fletching clearance is not a factor, these rests can have long, V-shaped launchers that cradle the arrow very securely. Though most drop-away rests don't contain the arrow as well as a capture rest prior to draw (there are exceptions), they do scoop up the arrow and hold it securely as soon as you start to draw.

Most drop-away rests follow a similar design scheme. They are not much different from conventional rests with their springs reversed and a cord attached between the launcher axle and the bow's harness system. In fact, the first drop-away rest I ever saw was on a target shooter's bow and he made it exactly this way — by modifying a conventional rest to make it snap down at the shot.

Some drop-away rests also capture the arrow so it can't fall off the rest at any time. Golden Key Futura's rests combine two of the best features available, drop away timing and full capture hold.

Some drop-away rests begin in the upright position and then drop after a cord attached to the bow's downward traveling harness draws taut at full draw. Most, however, start in the downward position and then the cord pulls them upward (against spring tension) during the draw and permits them to drop on release. The launcher rises and picks up the arrow as you draw the bow.

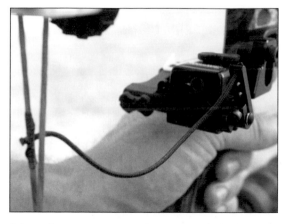

Most drop-away rests have a cord that is tied to the downward moving buss cable. This cord is also attached to the arrow launcher, which holds the arrow before flight. As the bow is drawn the cable is pulled down with the buss cable and that pulls the launcher up and positions your arrow to be shot.

IMPORTANCE OF REST TIMING

With nothing to support the arrow after the string is released, slight differences from one arrow to the next (nock straightness, arrow straightness, arrow spine) can cause the arrow to steer off course as the string speeds forward. Nock travel issues with the bow itself will also have a greater influence on the arrow when it is unsupported.

For this reason, it makes sense to set the rest to drop as late as possible during the shot — just in time to clear the fletching. The rest then offers some stability for the arrow and will tend to smooth out some of the differences from one arrow to the next.

Some drop-away rests feature a large hook that scoops up the arrow and centers it, no matter where it is lying on the rest shelf.

Rest Selection For Finger Shooters

When a finger shooter releases the bowstring, the first thing it does is move sideways to clear the fingertips. Then, it moves back in the other direction, toward the bow. This sets up a series of side-to-side oscillations in the string and arrow that causes it to flex sideways as it moves forward. A shaft that is properly matched to the bow's draw weight and draw length will curve out around the rest, with the tail end (and fletchings) following the string path which brings it in toward the riser and then back out again.

Ideally, the arrow curves perfectly around the rest, with minimal contact. Unfortunately, things aren't always perfect. The finger release is not the same as the consistent release you get from a release aid. It can and will change from time to time. Contact between the rest and the arrow's fletching is inevitable.

The best rests for finger shooters are designed to minimize the effects of contact. A forgiving rest that clears easily out of the fletching's path is required. Flipper rests with light spring tension are among the very best in this regard and the top choice of most accurate finger shooters. Also popular are simple "springy" rests. Because the arrow passes around these rests, they are called "shoot-around" rests.

Steve Johnson, inventor of the Spot-Hogg shooting machine, has tested drop-away rests on his machines using a high-speed camera. Steve has concluded that the greatest accuracy occurs for most bows when the rest supports the arrow for as long as possible before falling in time to clear the fletching. He recommends that each archer determine this point for himself by adjusting the cord length in small increments.

Drop-away rests permit you to shoot arrows with more helical offset without creating a tuning problem. This produces greater stability and accuracy when broadhead tipped hunting arrows are the ammunition of choice. If you are having a problem with fletching contact on your hunting rig, give these new rests a try.

LOOKING AHEAD

Without question, sights and rests are the most important accessories you need to select before you have a well set up bow, but there are a few odds and ends that also can improve accuracy. And with more than 75 percent of bowhunters using a release aid, these accessories also warrant some important consideration. In the next chapter, I'll get into the merits of the wrist sling, why most top shooters use them and why I don't. I'll also reveal several tradeoffs related to selecting the perfect release aid for bowhunting.

Chapter 17

SLINGS AND RELEASES

I've dedicated many years of my life to finding the most accurate method for releasing the bowstring. I'm here to tell you that if fingers were the best, I would have calluses like rawhide on my fingertips. But they're soft as a baby's behind. Instead, when I draw my bow, I have an old, worn mechanical release aid strapped around my wrist. This one has actually been there for 15 hunting seasons. If you aren't using a release aid, you're limiting your ability to shoot an arrow accurately. Here are five reasons why this should be the year you switch to a mechanical release.

Beat target panic: Target panic is the inability to hold the pin steady while aiming at the spot you want to hit. Invariably, those fighting the disease find

Tighter groups are one realistic expectation when shooting a mechanical release.

themselves twitching and lunging at the trigger as the pin approaches the spot. It's hard to beat target panic if you're a finger shooter. The cure seems more like psychiatric therapy than archery instruction. But, with a mechanical release, you can use a systematic method that doesn't rely as heavily on the archer's ability to control his or her nerves. You simply learn to squeeze the trigger slowly so the shot takes you by surprise.

Several of my buddies that switched from fingers to a mechanical release did so to beat target panic. In fact, come to think of it, I've never known a buddy who gave a release aid an honest try that later went back to releasing with fingers.

Easier tuning: When you release the string with fingers, it moves to the side as it clears your fingertips. This sets up a series of side-to-side oscillations of the bowstring and arrow. It is a tough tuning environment. On the other hand, arrows released with a mechanical release aid tend to travel much straighter leaving the bow, making it easier to achieve perfect arrow flight and maximum accuracy with fast arrows.

Shooting for 15 minutes three times a week will help you achieve acceptable hunting accuracy when using a mechanical release.

Less practice time: We all lead busy lives. No matter how much we may love to shoot a bow, it is hard to find the time to practice on a regular basis. It takes a lot of practice time to keep a finger release smooth and true. However, you can be a very good shot with a release aid shooting only 15 minutes a day three times per week. If you find it hard to shoot the number of arrows required to keep your fingers working together, you will be impressed with how easy it is to maintain acceptable accuracy with a release aid.

Better in the cold: If you've ever sat in a cold treestand for three or four hours when the temperature is below freezing and the wind is blowing 15 mph, you know cold weather performance is a big part of bowhunting. Regardless of the temperature, a release aid will drop the string the same way every time you pull the trigger. A good finger release relies on two or three fingers working together to get off the string the same way every time. When fingers get cold and stiff, they lose their feel and become less fluid. The possibility of making a poor release increases.

With a release aid, it is easier to make a good shot when wearing heavy gloves. Even a finger that's completely numb can still be commanded to curl — that's enough to get the job done with a release aid.

More accurate: I saved the most important reason for last. You'll discover greater accuracy with a release aid. It's an emotionless machine; as long as the trigger is pulled, it does the same thing every single time. Regardless of circumstance, it frees the string with amazing consistency. In archery, consistency is synonymous with accuracy.

If you are releasing the string with your fingers and are not totally satisfied with your accuracy — or if you're tired of fighting target panic — switch to a release aid. At first, the whole system will seem foreign, but after a couple of months, the release aid will feel

Release aids work well with warm gloves, whereas the finger release can be cumbersome in cold weather.

like an extension of your hand. Your newfound accuracy will astound you, and your confidence will soar. A confident hunter is a better hunter.

WRIST SLINGS

I am going to start out by saying I don't like wrist slings. I don't use them, and I probably never will. However, I am not taking super long shots each fall. My success generally is related to timing more than pure, hair-splitting accuracy. If I get the shot at the right time, as a big whitetail walks past my stand, I will do just fine. If I have to fumble my hand through a sling just to grab the bow, I am in trouble.

Releases that have adjustable lengths are easier to set up for accurate shooting. You want the release short enough that you can contact the trigger with the inside of your first knuckle.

Your bow sling represents the single greatest traffic jam in the race to full draw. It is very time consuming and distracting to have to work your gloved

---

Adjusting Trigger Pull

Adjust the trigger tension so that you can feel the trigger with gloved hands but not so heavy that you have to jerk it to get it to fire. A trigger pull similar to a shotgun trigger (not a hair trigger) will work best for most bowhunters.

Trigger pull adjustability is a quality all good releases share. Because the triggering mechanism relies upon a friction sear, bows with higher holding weights cause the release to have a stiffer trigger. In most cases, you can customize your release to the bow you shoot by simply turning an Allen wrench to increase or decrease the amount of trigger travel. Always start out with the release set too stiff and slowly turn the adjustment screw in until the perfect tension is achieved.

When comparing the trigger tension of a mechanical release to that of a gun, strive for a feel that is similar to what you get with a shotgun. Rifle-fine trigger tensions are not practical with the rough mechanisms found in most release aids. Trigger pulls of more than one pound are acceptable, and even higher tensions are common and will work. You want enough trigger tension so that you can feel it even with a gloved finger before the release fires.

Experiment with trigger tension after you get your release aid and determine the best tradeoff between surprise release performance and enough tension to permit you to feel the trigger through your warm gloves. This is one of the reasons why I always practice while wearing gloves, even during the middle of summer. I want to have perfect familiarity with the way the trigger will feel while hunting.

Selecting a Release Aid

There are many different styles of release aids. I will give only a short summary of each here along with the pros and cons. Choosing a release is a personal thing. Some people like a thumb trigger while others like an index finger trigger. Some like to hold the release in their hand while others like to have it attached securely to their wrist.

CALIPER RELEASES

Possibly the most popular hunting release, the caliper has a no nonsense design. It has all-manual operation with very few moving parts. In most cases, the jaws don't close by themselves when the string is engaged. You have to do that by flipping the trigger forward with your finger. You can find hand-held caliper releases, but most come attached to a wrist-strap.

Durability and reliability are the caliper's greatest strengths. Most are also very affordable. I've shot a bunch of arrows with caliper releases and I have yet to experience a misfire. The only problem with calipers, as well as almost all other wrist-strap releases, is the fact that they are always in the way. In some cases, you can turn the release around to the back of your hand if it is loose enough.

The basic two-jaw caliper is still the most popular style of release for hunting because it is trouble-free.

THREE-FINGER THUMB TRIGGER RELEASES

One of my bowhunting buddies shoots only three-finger releases because he loves the ability to clip the release on his string nocking loop and just leave it hanging there until a nice buck walks past. He is able to keep his hands free from the nuisance of an attached wrist-strap release, while at the same time avoiding the need to load the release onto the string during the moment of truth.

In my experience, it is harder to shoot heavy hunting weight bows with the three-finger design than with releases featuring a wrist strap. You must carry the entire draw weight with three fingers, causing more tension than I like. But that's just me. Those who are more accustomed to their use have found these releases to be extremely versatile and accurate. Make sure you keep an extra one in your fanny pack because they are easy to lose or drop from a tree stand.

HAND-HELD STRAP-ON RELEASES

Several bowhunters I know use releases that have a palm bar that you grip. The release straps around your hand and you trigger it with your index finger. These releases feel very secure and allow you to handle heavy hunting weight bows easily. One of the most popular examples of this release style is the Winn Free Flight. This simple and rugged design is attached to a strap-on glove with a palm bar for added power when drawing heavy hunting weight bows.

My only gripe with these releases is that they are always literally right in the palm of your hand. They make it hard to handle simple things like a grunt call or a cup of coffee. But, if that is the biggest complaint I can come up with, then these must be pretty good hunting releases, and they certainly are.

Some bowhunters favor thumb-trigger releases because they can leave them attached to the string and just grab the release when it is time to draw and shoot.

hand into the sling when you really need to be focusing on picking a shooting lane. To overcome this problem I practice shooting without a sling. I have taken to using only bows with narrow grip sections that permit me to completely encircle the riser without choking it. By coiling my fingers lightly around the grip, I can shoot with a surprise release method without fear of launching the bow right out of my hand.

For a wrist sling to work well, it must be snug to your wrist so that the bow becomes an extension of your hand. If it is loose, it will not serve its intended purpose.

Many bowhunters never actually benefit from their sling, because they don't make a surprise release. In other words, they don't need a sling. If you can shoot your bow with an "open hand" with total security without a sling, I have two comments. First, why would you ever want to use one? Second, your shooting form is not ideal since you are anticipating the moment of release so you can snap your hand closed. This can lead to target panic. The perfect shot should take you by surprise.

Those are my views. I know it is not enough to rely on just one side of the debate when it comes to equipment choices, so I asked Randy Ulmer his feelings on the subject of wrist slings. Not surprisingly, being a hardcore target shooter and a great long-range bowhunter, Randy had a different line of reasoning.

This is what Randy had to say: "A wrist sling is actually one of the most important accessories on your bow. With a sling, you can learn to use perfect form. To do that, the bow has to become part of your hand. Without a sling, you will have to manufacture a less than ideal grip or you will quickly start snapping your hand closed every time you shoot. That's no way to reach your potential.

"If you use proper release techniques while at the same time keeping your bow hand and all five fingers totally relaxed — like you should — you'll launch the bow every time if you don't use a wrist sling. Most wrist slings I see on bowhunters' bows are worthless. They are too loose. Your sling has to be snug. Ideally, it should be tight enough that you have to work your hand back and forth a few times inside the sling in order to get it to slide into place. You should feel like the sling is holding your hand in the grip. That will create the perfect marriage between bow and bow hand."

There is no debating that a sling will enhance pure accuracy if you have the time to use them. I have shot two bucks that each gave me only a few seconds from the time I first saw them until I had to shoot. I never could have gotten those shots if I had to snake my hand into a tight sling.

When choosing a bow sling, make sure you have enough adjustment so you can easily get your hand in and out of the grip.

If you decide to use a sling, look for one that gives you a secure feeling and one you can get your hand into as easily as possible. Simple braided leather slings are a good choice for bowhunting. Above all else, a wrist sling needs to give the feeling that the bow is attached to your hand. There should be no possible way you can drop the bow no matter how hard you try. That will encourage you to make a good surprise release with no subconscious attempt to anticipate when the shot will occur.

LOOKING AHEAD

I mentioned that your string is one of your most important accessories and your most overlooked. In the next chapter, I will take you through the string from loop to loop. It may not sound very exciting compared to buying sights and rests, but if you bear with me on this, I know I can make it worth your while.

Chapter 18

TAKE YOUR STRING SERIOUSLY

Despite getting no respect from even some very experienced archers, the string is quite possibly the most important accessory on your bow. It is one of the two things that actually contact your arrow (the rest is the other), and it has the most likelihood of being of low quality. Selecting a reliable string and caring for it properly is priority number one. If you take nothing else from this book beyond the need to own a good bowstring, my mission is accomplished.

Think about it, most sight pins don't move during the season. You can say the same of the vast majority of rests on the market. But, unfortunately, many bowstrings will change length continuously for the first year or two after you buy the bow; sometimes indefinitely. And those changes will destroy your accuracy and confidence.

There is no question standard-issue strings are getting better, but it is still common to fight a twisting, stretching string at some point during the season. I see time bombs — especially in the form of sloppy center serving — ticking away on the bows of several of the guys

A high-quality bowstring is a requirement — not a luxury.

I hunt with every season.

The fact that one of the most important accessories on your bow is prone to change without warning should leave you feeling a bit uneasy. Don't ignore your string.

MATERIALS

Let's start by understanding the differences in the basic materials used to make the fibers. These are all synthetics, and they fall into two categories: light-weight, elastic fibers (Spectra and Dyneema are two trade names) and heavier, stiffer, inelastic fibers (Vectran). Spectra and Dyneema can be used in their pure form for strings and harnesses, but Vectran has to be blended with one of these in order to function properly.

Spectra and Dyneema are both made from beads of polyethylene and have low melting points in the range of 160 degrees Fahrenheit. Vectran is a synthetic with a much higher melting point (400 to 500 degrees) and is much more resistant to creep than either Spectra or Dyneema. However, pure Vectran is brittle and can break with little warning.

While zero creep and a high melting point are qualities that make Vectran a good choice for strings and harnesses, its lack of durability and elasticity essentially disqualifies it from being used in its pure state. Also, Vectran absorbs wax more readily than Spectra or Dyneema and is therefore heavier, producing somewhat slower arrow speeds.

Fiber makers have learned that by combining Dyneema or Spectra with Vectran in varying rates, they can get the best of both worlds: an acceptably durable fiber that doesn't creep over time. Many of today's top bow companies and string makers prefer these "blended" fibers for this reason. This is especially important with single-cam bows that essentially have a double length string with twice the potential for stretch.

BCY and Brownell are the two primary makers of synthetic strands for the manufacture of bowstrings and harnesses. Both companies are continually experimenting with new formulas and processes to fine-tune their products.

Ultra-Cam is the newest fiber from Brownell (www.brownellarchery.com). It is a Dyneema/Vectran blend that has been formulated to reduce stretch while still maintaining good performance and durability. It is very thin in diameter, a quality that permits more fibers to be used when creating a string or harness. The result is a bundle that is pleasingly round in shape that fits better in the grooves of a cam. Brownell also makes several other excellent fibers for compound bow shooters; including Fast Flight (Spectra), S4 and S4 Thin (Spectra/Vectran blend) and D75 and D75 Thin (Dyneema), TS Plus and Xcel (another blend).

BCY (www.bcyfibers.com) offers four basic options for the string maker; 450 Plus, 452 and 452X, which are Dyneema/Vectran blends of varying diameter. DynaFlight 97 and Formula 8125 are made of Dyneema, the biggest difference being the smaller diameter of Formula 8125.

While blends are very useful for harnesses, many bow companies and cus-

BCY offers some of the finest bowsting material available today. Whether you pre-fer Dyneema, Spectra or a Vectran blend, BCY Fibers has exactly what you need.

tom string makers manufacture their strings from pure Dyneema or Spectra. These unblended fibers have improved greatly in recent years to make them more stable and resistant to stretch. They work well for bows of average draw weight and they are a bit faster and quieter than strings made of blended fibers.

Thankfully, you don't have to understand all the material specs to shoot your bow accurately, but someone has to or your string will stretch. Just keep in mind that there are materials and technologies out there right now that virtually eliminate string and harness stretch. Don't be satisfied with a stretchy string, and don't be afraid to ask a few questions when buying a new bow or string to determine whether it is a high-quality product. You may pay a bit more for the best, but it is a good investment that will repay you many times over in the years to come.

CHOOSING A STRING

This chapter begs the question: how can I tell what I am getting? That is a very tough question to answer. I know which companies are using good strings and harnesses, but that is only because I have owned and shot just about everything on the market. And it changes every year as companies continually upgrade.

When buying a new string and harness system, or a new bow, it is worth asking many questions about stretch resistance. But there are other things you can do. Look at the string itself. If it has a monofilament center serving, it is old and very likely made using yesterday's technology. Avoid those strings.

Also, look at the center serving closely, even if it is made of a braided material. Today's best strings use super tight, braided synthetic serving to reduce slip and improve wear life. If the serving looks solid and tight, chances are better the string was made with pre-stretched fibers and the serving applied tightly — the mark of quality.

Finally, you can look at the cam or cams. You will need to know what their proper rotation looks like in order to know if the string has stretched since it was installed. The archery shop attendant may know, or you may have to call the bow maker's customer service department to find out. If the string has obviously stretched since the bow was made, it is not a high quality string. You can expect it to keep stretching for months, maybe for as long as you own the bow.

In the end, the only sure test is experience. If your string stretches noticeably over the first few weeks you own the bow, you should think about replacing it with a custom, pre-stretched string and then tell all your friends that the company you bought your bow from didn't supply you with a useable string. The dollar votes, and if enough people demand quality strings, this problem will disappear.

When buying a new string or even a new bow, asking the pro shop salesman about string quality is just the starting point. You should look over the string yourself and check to see if the center serving is tightly wrapped. Also, check over the cams to assure timing is accurate. You might need to call the manufacturer for the correct positioning of the cams. If the bow is new and the string has already stretched just sitting there, you can assume the string isn't of the highest quality.

HOW TO TELL IF YOU HAVE A PROBLEM

String stretch causes your cam or cams to rotate. The easiest way to tell if you have a stretch problem is to mark your cam or cams (not your idler wheel if you shoot a single-cam bow) with white paint in a way that allows you to line the limb up with the cam and check its rotation. When you have the bow set up the way you like it, make a dot on the cam that lines up with the limb. You can tell immediately in the future when the string stretches and the cam rotates.

THE CUSTOM STRING SOLUTION

While the quality of the average string that comes with a bow is improving each year, some still fall woefully short of perfection. Some only stretch a small amount, while others creep an inch, or more, over the first few months of service. This requires a level of monitoring and maintenance most bowhunters find far too tedious. I'm one of them. I don't want my accuracy to depend on anything that changes over time.

Additionally, most standard-issue strings have a loose center serving that you have to replace immediately after the bow is broken in (after 75 percent of the string creep has already occurred). This is a time-consuming chore. Again, it's tedium at best and an unrecognized problem at worst.

And then there's peep sight rotation. As a string creeps and settles, the rotation of the peep changes. You have to take the time to visit the archery shop or remove and twist the string several times while setting up a bow just to get the peep to settle in — or live with an ill-trained peep. And if your hunting season stretches over months instead of weeks, you may find yourself having to tweak the peep during the season. I just don't like any of this stuff. Strings are very serious business, and you can't take them for granted.

A good, pre-stretched custom bowstring and harness system, that either comes with a quality bow or that you buy separately and put on your bow after you buy it, will solve these problems. It is one of the best investments you can make to assure your bow doesn't change impact point during the season. I now rely on these carefully made string and harness systems on every bow I take

Some cams have laser engraved timing marks to assure the cams are rotating properly and timing is correct.

Diffusing a Ticking Time Bomb

I was helping a friend set up a new bow a couple of summers back. I was rushed for time, so we did all the easy stuff: put on the rest, sight, nocking point and peep. On the surface, everything looked fine, but I knew better. When I handed him the bow, I told him I'd be seeing him again pretty soon. He looked at me somewhat funny but didn't ask any questions. I knew my friend's string serving was a ticking time bomb that would derail his enthusiasm within a week or two. You can tell by the texture, color and shape of a serving whether it is tight. Like many on the market at that time, this one looked loose.

I was shooting with Larry 10 days later when his arrows started soaring over the target and into the woods. He was distraught. Larry is always full of trash talk and a general pain in the behind at times, so trying not to laugh too loud, I just let him suffer for a few rounds. Finally, I felt the slightest compassion and stepped in. It was immediately obvious that the serving had slipped down. Generally, serving slips up but this time it went the other way. I finally had to take the time to do what I knew I'd eventually have to do anyway: reserve Larry's bowstring.

A quality center serving jig is necessary for tight wraps. Pictured is BCY's Bearpaw Bowstring Serving Tool. It features an adjustable tension control and stainless steel rollers.

Most serious archers quickly learn that one of the first things they must do when they buy a new bow with a typical string is remove the serving and replace it properly. Monofilament serving doesn't have enough abrasion resistance or breaking strength to stand up to repeated shots with a release aid, and factory-installed braided synthetic serving is almost always too loose. It will soon slip.

String stretch is one of the biggest reasons for serving slip on properly served bows. As the string stretches, it draws thinner and the serving separates, opening up gaps — generally right where you attach your release aid or tie your nocking loop. This exposes the string to damage and obviously results in the nock point moving.

Experts in the art of string making have told me that a string must be twisted before serving in order to hold the serving tight. The recommended amount of twist is roughly one turn per inch. Since most factory strings stretch during the break-in period anyway, shoot a couple hundred arrows from the bow before deciding if you have to replace the serving. If the string has stretched, make sure to add a few twists to return it to its proper length. There is more information about the techniques for serving a string in Chapter 4.

hunting. It has made getting a new bow ready for the season much easier.

Every year, more companies come on the market offering pre-stretched custom strings, which they build under high tension to further eliminate creep. You have plenty of options and the price is coming down, so shop around. Thankfully, you live in a time when you can shop easily from your computer using the Internet. Put this resource to good use finding an affordable, high-quality string and harness for your bow if it doesn't already have one.

MAINTAINING YOUR STRING AND HARNESS SYSTEM

A well-made string will be stable and will not twist when you draw the bow. Your peep should remain in the correct rotation.

By routinely waxing your string and harness system with a good wax, you accomplish four objectives: lubricate the fibers and prevent "fiber to fiber" abrasion, keep the bundle of strands together, maintain and extend the life of the string and help prevent water absorption. After applying the wax to the string, rub it rapidly with your fingers to heat the wax so it flows into the cracks of the string. Some fibers have a low melting point so don't get carried away.

Don't take strings and harnesses for granted; they are the primary cause of unexpected changes in accuracy. There are a number of good custom string makers on the market that will help you choose the best system to eliminate this problem. If it's time to replace the string and harness on your bow, consider upgrading to a high-quality setup using today's high-tech synthetics. You'll be surprised by how much difference it can make.

Maintain your string in good working condition by waxing it regularly.

LOOKING AHEAD

If you thought there were many options in the rest, sight and string markets, just wait until you turn the page. I can have you going from lobbing to zipping in one simple step. The ultimate in fine-tuning of any hunting bow comes with selecting the right arrow. That is where our journey takes us in the next chapter.

Chapter 19

MODERN ARROW SELECTION

T here are many things to consider when selecting arrows. The old argument of carbon versus aluminum is pretty much dead. Carbon won that battle a few years ago. Very few serious archery hunters are still using aluminum arrows. They are economical, but carbon has so many other advantages going for it that it is hard to select anything else. When deciding what arrows to buy, here are a few things to consider.

WHY CARBON

I mentioned that carbon arrows are much more popular among archery hunters than aluminum arrows. Here are several reasons why.

Wind drift: If you hunt in areas where the wind blows, a small diameter arrow will improve accuracy. Today's smallest diameter aluminum/carbon composite arrows are roughly $^{15}/_{64}$ inches in diameter. Compare that to roughly $^{24}/_{64}$ inches for a popular 2413 aluminum arrow. A 28-inch small diameter composite shaft has a side profile with an area of 6.56 square inches. The 2413 has a side profile area of roughly 10.5 square inches —

For most bowhunting situations, arrows with a straightness of +/- .005 or .006 inches are sufficient.

When shooting in windy conditions, an arrow with small fletching and a thin diameter will drift less than one with a large diameter and large fletchings.

1.6 times greater.

When you shoot small diameter arrows into a crosswind, they exhibit less sideways drift than larger diameter arrows because there is less surface area against which the wind can push. If you forget to account for the wind, these smaller diameter arrows are better able to bail you out at typical bowhunting distances.

By switching from large diameter aluminum arrows to small diameter carbon arrows with the same four-inch fletching, you can literally cut your wind drift in half on 40-yard shots.

Feather Waterproofing

New waterproofing powders promise much better performance for feather fletching than the silicone-based foam carpet sealer I used 15 years ago. I've seen some dramatic demonstrations of the effectiveness of these new powders. Simply dump some powder into a plastic sandwich bag, insert the fletched end of your arrow and give it a vigorous shaking. You're set for tough hunting conditions. Two good sources of waterproofing powder are Gateway Feathers (www.gatewayfeathers.com) and Bohning Archery (www.bohning.com).

Down range arrow speed: Due to friction with the air, arrows slow down the farther they get from the bow. The greater the surface area of an arrow, the more drag it experiences and the faster it slows down. I set up a test that explored this phenomenon. Using two chronographs, I tested the speed of the arrow right out of the bow and again at 40 yards. At 40 yards, small diameter carbon arrows lose about seven percent of their initial speed while a 2312 aluminum arrow (of the same weight) loses 8.4 percent of its initial speed. Granted, this is not a huge difference, but bowhunting is a tough game and I'll take every advantage I can get.

Durability: Carbon arrows are more durable than aluminum arrows. They are more resilient and can take more abuse without bending or cracking.

Straightness: Because you can straighten aluminum tubes but not carbon tubes, aluminum arrows tend to be straighter than carbon arrows. In order to maintain a high straightness standard with carbon arrows, the manufacturer has to test and cull the best shafts from a production run. That adds cost to the product. You can get extremely straight carbon arrows, but they will be more expensive.

When you combine aluminum and carbon in one arrow, you get the best of both construction materials. You get the durability of carbon and the straightness of aluminum. These composite arrows tend to be very expensive too.

The obvious question is: How straight do my arrows need to be for hunting? An arrow that is straight to +/- .005 inch (the common standard for carbon arrows) is more than adequate for any bowhunting

Arrows made of a combination of carbon and aluminum such as Easton's Axis Full Metal Jacket have a smaller diameter that promotes penetration and reduces wind drift.

situation. You absolutely won't notice a difference between an arrow that is +/- .003-inch versus one that is +/- .006 inch. It is like splitting hairs.

Penetration: In all the testing I've seen and done, small diameter carbon arrows penetrated better than larger diameter aluminum arrows of the same weight. Though stiffness may play some role, diameter appears to be the greatest reason that carbon shafts do so well in these tests. Reducing surface area reduces resistance as the shaft slips into the target. The tests I have witnessed concluded that carbon arrows penetrate anywhere from 15 to 40 percent deeper than the same weight aluminum. The variation in results is related to the diameter of the arrows in the comparison.

SELECTING THE RIGHT SIZE

Selecting the right size is easy. You simply call the arrow manufacturer or go onto their website for sizing guidelines. You merely need to know your bow's maximum draw weight and your arrow length to select the correct size. Size is really stiffness. A heavy bow or one shooting a long arrow needs to shoot stiff arrows in order to achieve good arrow flight.

This is not to suggest that you don't have options. Man, do you have options. You can find arrows of the correct stiffness (size) for your bow weighing anywhere from five to nine grains per pound of your bow's maximum draw length. By looking at several manufacturers' products, and even within a single manufacturer's line, you will find many options to allow you to fine-tune your bow for the perfect combination of speed, penetration and silence.

ARROW WEIGHT

A bow's efficiency drops off fast when you start to use light arrows. For example, if the bow's efficiency drops five percent when you reduce your arrow weight from eight grains per pound of draw force (480 grains for a 60-pound bow) to six grains per pound (360 grains for a 60-pound bow) that doesn't mean it will be another 2.5 percent less efficient when you drop from six grains per pound to five grains per pound. The loss will be much higher; to the tune of 10 to 15 percent.

As your bow loses efficiency, two bad things happen. First, the bow will become much

In the author's penetration tests, smaller diameter carbon arrows out penetrated larger diameter aluminum arrows of equal weight.

louder. Second, penetration decreases because the energy in the arrow is reduced — less of the bow's energy makes it into the arrow.

There is a balance between arrow speed on one side and reliability and penetration on the other. At normal ranges out to 30 yards, a mid-weight arrow is fast enough to produce a trajectory that creates a clean kill even if you misjudge the distance by five yards. Granted, if you are taking a long shot at pronghorn antelope on the wide-open plains, you could benefit from a still flatter trajec-

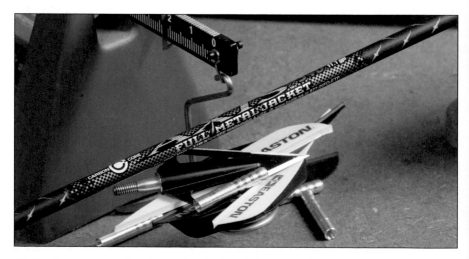

Strive for an arrow having a finished weight of roughly 6 to 6.5 grains for each pound of your bow's maximum draw weight.

Arrow Balance Point

The term Forward of Center, or FOC, describes an arrow's balance point. Balance point affects stability, so it is worth understanding this concept. You arrive at FOC by making a few measurements and then running the numbers through a simple formula.

Balance point: Install your broadhead and then find the arrow's balance point by sliding it back and forth along an edge. You'll find the spot where the arrow just balances. Mark it carefully. Now measure from the bottom of the nock groove to the balance point and write this number down.

Overall length: There are different conventions for measuring overall arrow length depending upon the type of point you are using.

Arrow balance is not something most bowhunters consider and it is not super critical on shots of moderate range, but to ensure maximum stability, keep your broadhead weight approximately equal to one-third of your shaft weight.

Arrows that include inserts: Measure from the bottom of the nock groove to the end of the arrow not including the insert. This is often referred to as the arrow's cut length.

Shafts with swaged tips: The overall length is measured from the bottom of the nock groove to the most forward extension of the full diameter of the shaft, just behind the swage.

Shafts that include outserts: Measure from the nock groove to a point three quarter inches forward of the rearward end of the outsert.

Shafts with glue-on heads: Measure from the nock groove to the most rearward portion of the glue-on point.

Determine FOC: To find the FOC, divide the overall length by two. This should produce the physical center of the shaft. Now subtract this number from the balance point and divide by the overall length. Multiply by 100 to express the fractional value as a percentage.

Most expert archers agree that an FOC value between seven and 10 percent will produce the best compromise between stability and a flat trajectory. If your FOC is too high, you can reduce your point weight or increase fletching weight. If your FOC is too low, do the opposite. FOC is just one factor affecting accuracy. Don't get too concerned about the exact number. As a rule of thumb, your broadhead should equal roughly one-third of the weight of your arrow shaft. For example, a 100-grain broadhead and a 300-grain shaft will produce a well-balanced finished arrow.

tory to reduce the effects of a similar 15 percent miscue in range estimation, but when shots are that long, there is generally less urgency and you have time to use your rangefinder.

Based on this logic, the perfect arrow for most bowhunting is one that has a finished weight of roughly 6.5 grains per pound of draw force. This arrow weight strikes the best overall balance between a trajectory flat enough to keep you in the kill zone out to 30 yards and a weight that's heavy enough to produce good penetration and quiet shooting.

At this arrow weight, a 70-pound, 30-inch draw length bow will shoot about 20 to 30 fps slower than its rated IBO speed. Of course, as you decrease draw weight and draw length, your speed will also drop slightly.

S tart with a dozen arrows. Ideally, they are brand new, but if you can't afford to buy a fresh dozen, at least spring for six new shafts. Number each arrow. Start with a clean target and put field points on your arrows. Shoot all of them at the paper at your maximum accurate range. Don't look

By numbering your arrows, you can keep track of where each arrow is hitting the target and remove those that don't impact with the others.

at the numbers as you shoot the arrows. When you go to pull them, write the corresponding number next to each hole.

Shoot every arrow at least six times and then look at the target to see if any patterns are forming. You will likely have several arrows that are consistently flying wide. Typically, I find that two-thirds of my arrows fly in the same hole, while one-third hit too far from the center to be acceptable. Obviously, I cull the loose grouping arrows out of my quiver before the season.

I'll save you a trip for the calculator. If you shoot 60 pounds, your finished arrow weight should be roughly 390 to 420 grains and if you shoot 70 pounds, your finished arrow weight should be 455 to 490 grains.

FLETCHING STYLE

Knowing when plastic is better than feathers and when five-inch fletching is better than four, or three or two, and when right helical is better than left, will allow you to fine-tune your arrow flight and hunting accuracy. Here are the trade-offs.

Why choose feathers: Feather fletching offers greater forgiveness of slight contact with the arrow rest. With today's full capture and drop-away rests, contact is

not a big issue. I have shot feather fletching in the past, but I can't come up with a case for them now.

However, if you release the string with fingers and use a shoot-around rest like a springy or flipper rest (the best choice for finger shooters), feather fletching makes more sense. In most cases, it is not possible to completely eliminate contact when releasing the string with fingers, so a fletching that forgives contact is definitely the ticket. Feather fletching is also a must for traditional archers resting their arrow on the shelf of a recurve or longbow.

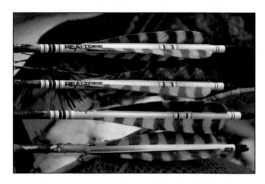

For compound shooters who shoot fingers, feather fletching is their best choice. Feathers slide easier past rest arms and prongs than plastic vanes. The only trade-off is they're less durable than plastic.

Why choose vanes: I use vanes instead of feathers for a number of reasons. Primarily, feathers are noisy in the quiver and they're noisier than new, clean vanes in flight. Noise is an archery hunter's enemy. Unless you use a good waterproofing powder, feathers also collapse when they get wet. They lose their ability to steer the arrow. Feathers are not very durable. You'll replace your feathers three times for every time you replace your vanes.

Also, with today's rests, you can use a stiffer, high profile vane and increase arrow stability without increasing the likelihood of fletching to rest contact.

FLETCHING ORIENTATION

You can select feathers or vanes, straight fletch, helical or four fletch at 105x75 degree spacing in eight different lengths, 20 different colors and 10 different shapes from a dozen different manufacturers with their own proprietary materials. There are literally hundreds of possible combinations when fletching your arrows, but we can keep this really simple. If you are a release aid shooter, use three helical offset vanes, four inches long. If you are a finger shooter, use three five-inch helical feathers.

Plastic vanes are a great option because they are very durable and weather resistant. Most archery hunters prefer four-inch vanes, such as those pictured here.

Amount of helical: Under hunting conditions, you are always better off with as much arrow stability as you can get. You get maximum stability by using fletching set to an aggressive helical offset. This setup will create maximum drag and spin to bring a poorly released hunting arrow under control fast.

Most commercially fletched helical arrows have between two and five degrees of offset in the helical. Easton's technical reps recommend four degrees. This designation refers to the angle the fletching makes with the shaft's centerline. Smaller diameter carbon shafts will not tolerate as much offset because the fletching clamps don't wrap the fletching around the shaft tightly.

My advice is to use the greatest amount of helical offset your fletching jig (or the one at the archery shop making your arrows) can produce while still maintaining the proper contact between the base of the fletching and the shaft.

Fletching length: Five-inch fletchings were the standard for hunting arrows just a few years ago, but shorter, stiffer, high-profile vanes are taking their place. As a good compromise, four-inch vanes are a fine choice. If you want to go shorter, two-inch, high-profile or fast spinning vanes are also a good choice.

Let's keep this simple. Here is my overall arrow recommendation for the major-

Use the most aggressive helical offset that your fletching clamp will permit while still producing proper adhesion to the arrow.

ity of archers using a release aid. Choose carbon arrows of the correct size having a weight of 6 to 6.5 grains per pound of maximum draw weight. Set them up with as much right helical offset as you can apply to four-inch plastic vanes. Experiment with some of today's fast spinning vanes, such as New Archery Products' Quik-Spin, for greater stability and I am sure you won't be disappointed. If you are a finger shooter, this arrow may work well, or you can substitute feathers for vanes to be on the safe side.

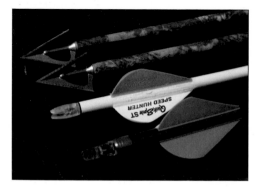

Short, stiff, high-profile vanes such as New Archery Products' QuikSpin Speed Hunter and Bohning's two-inch Blazer are becoming increasingly popular.

LOOKING AHEAD

Now you have your arrow. The next step is to choose a broadhead to go on the end. We think in terms of bows and arrows, but the broadhead is the part of the entire system that actually kills the animal, so it is important to have complete confidence in your heads. I have shot mechanical heads for many years with great satisfaction. In the next chapter, I'll tell you why I like them and what I would shoot if I were to switch back to a fixed-blade this year.

Chapter 20

CHOOSING A BROADHEAD

W ithout question, you can apply physics, testing and common sense to the decision of which broadhead to shoot. But in the end, the outcome will rely on emotion. Broadheads are the part that actually kills the game and thus there are as many different opinions as there are bowhunters.

Everyone has had a range of experiences with their broadheads. They may blame a poor shot on their heads when it was really caused by something completely different. Or, they may attribute their success to their heads when any head that would stay in one piece could have cleanly killed the animal. It doesn't matter. This is an emotional subject.

I have never gotten into a heated argument in hunting camp about which bow is the best, but I have certainly been in a number of them when it comes to broadheads.

In this chapter, I hope to cut through the emotion (I have my own biases, of course) and get down to the physics of arrow flight and an understanding of the trade-offs we are making. I hope when you are done reading this you will view broadhead selection with a different, more open-minded attitude.

The broadhead is the actual part responsible for the kill, and choosing your next head is as important as your next arrow or rest.

MECHANICAL HEADS

I consider myself conservative when it comes to equipment selection, a slow adopter, but I have never felt uncomfortable about mechanical heads. Here is why I like them.

Accuracy is the most important goal of any shot — whether at a target or at game. That has to be priority number one. I have talked with many broadhead makers over the years, and even those who didn't make mechanical heads stated that any broadhead that stays more or less in one piece will kill a deer-sized animal if you hit it in the right place.

Mechanical heads with a cutting diameter of 1.25 inches and short blades are perfect for big-game animals such as deer.

So, hitting them in the right place is obviously a big deal — dare I say, the biggest deal? There are many fixed-blade heads that fly nearly as well as field points under a wide range of conditions, but back in 1995 when I made the switch to mechanicals, there weren't any. I fought to achieve good accuracy on shots past 25 yards with the fixed-blade heads of the day. My biggest problems occurred with bows that were a bit quirky (some of those bows were impossible to tune) and when shooting in the wind. Achieving accuracy with fast arrows was a huge challenge. I spent many days each year tweaking and making tiny changes to improve my accuracy.

When I first began trying mechanical heads, taking them to the field to use on live game was a no-brainer. My accuracy was so much more consistent; my confidence surged. Knowing you will hit where you are aiming is huge.

More than a decade later, I am sure I have shot well over 200 big-game animals (I shoot does everywhere I hunt) with mechanical heads. My recovery rate has been very high. I can't think of a single shot I would take again with a different head. I have never had reason to question the effectiveness of the mechanical heads I have used. I'm sure there are situations where they are inferior to fixed-blade heads, but I have not encountered those situations personally.

As a qualifier to the previous paragraph, it is worth noting that I shoot conservative heads with relatively small (1.25-inch) cutting diameters and short blades that open easily upon impact. These heads don't affect penetration adversely (I've done the tests) and I have never seen them pole-vault (a phenomenon similar to skipping a rock, that supposedly occurs on angled hits). I shoot heavy arrows, so that might also contribute to the performance of these heads.

So much for personal experience, now let's look at the physics. Anytime you put a wing at the front of a projectile, you have the potential for steering. That is exactly what you are doing when you attach a fixed-blade broadhead to your arrow.

You work hard to figure out how best to shoot a bow and you tinker with the

Penetration Tests

I set up a test in which my dad shot 19 broadheads into foam and into a hardened mix of lard and Crisco to determine which heads penetrated best. We even put a thick chamois skin across the front of the block to assure that the blades opened on impact.

It was interesting to note that the best penetrating head in the test was a mechanical head. It had short blades and a cutting diameter of 1.25 inches, so it was a conservative design. Not surprisingly, I now hunt with that head. Several other small cutting diameter mechanical heads penetrated on par with the fixed blade heads we tested. We didn't test two-blade cut-on-contact heads, but they likely would have penetrated best of all.

It is interesting that we actually started with 20 models; one mechanical model fell apart almost every time we shot it into the lard/Crisco blend, even though we used new heads for every shot. Happily, that head is no longer on the market. Heads like that are the reason mechanical broadheads received a bad name.

You may have reasons to avoid mechanical broadheads, but penetration should not be one of them. As long as you choose modest heads with cutting diameters between 1⅛ and 1¼ inches, they penetrate just as well as fixed-blade broadheads of the same size when shot directly into the target.

tuning until you have great arrow flight. Now, the last thing you want is an arrow that decides on its own which way it will go once it leaves the bow. With a wing at the front, there is always that potential. The larger the wing, the larger the potential problem. I'm not saying a problem is guaranteed. When you have a well-tuned bow, a perfectly straight arrow, with a nock, insert and broadhead all in alignment, and when you hold good shooting form through the shot, you will shoot most fixed-blade heads accurately. But if any of those elements breaks down, you will have a wind-planing issue. And the faster it flies, the more it will wind-plane.

Before diving head deep into broadhead tuning, be sure to sight in your bow with field points and get your centershot and nock height adjusted.

If you remove the wing from the front of the arrow, or reduce the size of the wing, you eliminate or reduce the possibility for a problem. That is Aerodynamics 101.

The goal then becomes a combination of two tasks. First, make the wing as small as possible. Second, get the bow, arrow and your shooting form as good as possible. The smallest wing is no wing, and that is the only reason I shoot mechanical broadheads.

Selecting the best size: I want a small mechanical head that opens to roughly 1.25 to 1.5 inches. I can understand why you might want a bigger style and I have spoken with many die-hard bowhunters who use mechanicals that open to two inches, or more.

My arrows possess enough energy to shoot a mechanical that opens up to six inches, like a pair of steak knives. That would be great on soft-tissue hits, but when I do have a slight bauble and hit the animal in the shoulder, I still need penetration. You get better penetration with smaller heads. I want to be able to kill a deer that I accidentally shoot in the shoulder. With a smaller head, I increase the odds of a clean kill.

How it opens matters. When a mechanical head opens from the back forward, it acts more like a fixed-blade head on impact. Less of the arrow's energy is needed to open the blades and more is available to penetrate the animal. If the blades open from the front back (the way most of them do), the shorter blades used in the smaller designs I favor will not rob as much energy.

Mechanical heads are definitely a good choice for those who want the most accurate head, but they aren't as durable as fixed-blade heads. Because the blades of a mechanical head are unsupported, it is easier for them to break on a bone hit.

FIXED-BLADE BROADHEADS

We need to go back to the analogy of the wing on the front of the arrow. If we make the wing smaller, it has less potential to steer the arrow. That is why I like the new category of fixed-blade heads that have dominated the market during the past three years. They have short, compact blades with high blade angles.

Fixed cut-on-contact broadheads penetrate better than any other style of head on the market, making them a popular style of head. They're great for youth and women who shoot lower poundages, and for bowhunters looking to get the most penetration possible out of their bow setups.

Replaceable-blade broadheads are perfect for the hunter who doesn't like sharpening blades every year or who can't afford to buy new broadheads each year. New Archery Products' Thunderhead is one of the top selling replaceable-blade broadheads today.

Like mechanical broadheads with short blades, they create more of a chopping effect than a slicing effect.

Most of us can live with a chopping effect as long as the head hits where we aim. That is the strength of these heads; by reducing the amount of blade surface area, they fly better under a wider range of conditions and at higher arrow speeds.

Here are a few examples of this style of broadhead. There are many on the market now, and I will probably miss a few, but you will at least get the idea. Look at the New Archery Products Nitron, Muzzy MX-3, Slick Trick, American Broadheads Sonic, Wac' Em, Aftershock Maniac, Steel Force Sabertooth HP, Tight Point Shuttle T-Lock, Rocky Mountain Blitz, Grim Reaper Hades, G5 Striker, Rocket Bunker Buster, Wasp Boss and Innerloc Stainless Extreme. Cut-to-the-point versions include the Magnus Stinger and the NAP Hell Razor.

These are just some of the newest heads on the market. The list is in no way comprehensive. There are literally dozens of fixed-blade broadhead models. Not only can you choose between several different styles of replaceable-blade heads, but you can also choose between several different styles of cut-on-contact one-piece heads. The choices can seem bewildering, but I will try to bring a little order to the trade-offs so you can see through the fog of options.

Style: As mentioned, you can choose between one-piece cut-on-contact heads or replaceable-blade heads. Both styles have their advantages. Recently, the cut-on-contact heads have really improved to the point where they will fly well even from fast compound bows. There is no reason not to try them. It is the perfect choice if your number one goal is penetration. A two-bladed, cut-on-contact head will penetrate better than anything else on the market, bar none.

Replaceable-blade heads are obviously easier for the majority of bowhunters to use, because you don't need to sharpen the blades. When blades become dull or overly used, simply replace the blades with new ones. Most replaceable-blade heads have three blades, some have four blades and a very few have two blades.

Cutting diameter: Cutting diameter creates another trade-off. A large cutting diameter means more surface to potentially steer the arrow offline if you are using a fixed-blade head. However, on impact, especially with soft tissue,

Cut-on-contact broadheads require sharpening skills to get that killing edge sharp before hunting season arrives. After practicing, be sure and touch up the blades for the best penetration.

having a large cutting diameter increases the chances for a quick kill. Each person must make this decision for themselves, but if I were going to shoot fixed-blade heads again, I would shoot those with cutting diameters in the 1.25-inch range — or even slightly smaller.

Number of blades: The more blades the head has, the less it will penetrate. This is because every blade encounters resistance when it cuts into the animal. The more blades, the more resistance. Beyond a certain point, you gain very little tissue damage by increasing the number of blades. I don't see much value in shooting heads with more than three blades. The only exception is cut-on-contact heads with two primary blades and two smaller, bleeder blades. In this case, a four-bladed head makes sense.

If you know you are going to make a perfect hit, the broadhead you choose isn't important. It only has to be sharp. However, making a perfect hit is where the challenge lies. First, you need to figure out how you will make it and then you have to reduce the downside if you don't. Those are the two big issues when selecting broadheads.

Strive to choose a broadhead that lets you zip your hunting arrows just as accurately as your field point tipped practice arrows. While accuracy is priority number one, it is never guaranteed. If you choose carefully, you will also end up with a head that offers all the penetration you need to make good on a shoulder hit.

LOOKING AHEAD

That wraps up the equipment selection portion of this book. I'm guessing you are mopping your brow now, trying to digest all these options and variables. I hope I offered enough guidance that you were able to make solid choices to complement the way you hunt. In the next section of this book, I'll get into the art and science of tuning your setup for the very best arrow flight and ultimate accuracy. Read on, there is still much to learn.

Chapter 21

TUNING SIMPLIFIED

I learned to ride a bicycle when I was about 6 years old. My dad got me on the sparkling green Schwinn Sting Ray and pushed me down a hill in our lawn. I was nervous and a little scared, but mostly I feared I simply couldn't do it. After two or three glides across the lawn, I was on cloud nine. It was much easier than I had expected, and I laughed at my former trepidation. How could I have been so worried about something that, once conquered, seemed so easy?

Tuning a bow is much like riding a bicycle or any number of other small milestones we achieve that seem so difficult when looking out the windshield of life but so easy in the rear view mirror. Once you get past the fear that tuning is some kind of black magic you will never understand, you will be like I was a few decades ago, whooping and hollering across the lawn on my fancy new bike. Well, maybe that

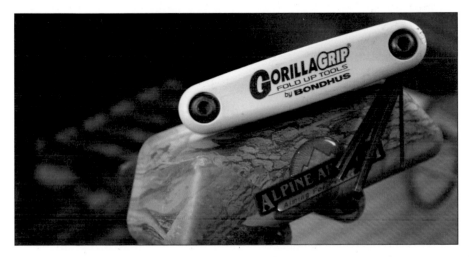

Learning to tune your own bow will pay big dividends in your performance. To start off, you must own a good set of Allen wrenches.

is a little melodramatic, but you get the picture. You will look back and say, "Wow, that was a lot easier than I thought it would be."

LIKE THROWING A PAPER AIRPLANE

This analogy will help you understand how adjustments to your bow and arrow will affect arrow flight. I'll start with a question. At a range of 15 feet, would you rather try to hit a small target with a dart or a paper airplane?

That's easy: we would all take the dart, of course. For the same reasons a dart flies better than a paper airplane, a field-point equipped practice arrow is easier to shoot accurately than one carrying a broadhead. That is why tuning is so important. Though a poorly flying arrow will plane offline slightly even without a broadhead attached (the amount it veers is small), it really takes off when you attach a broadhead.

When you throw a dart, it really doesn't matter which way it's pointing when it leaves your hand. With its aerodynamic tip and its stabilizing tail fins, it quickly rights itself and flies straight. A paper airplane, on the other hand, is a lot tougher to throw in a straight line. Unless everything is perfect, as soon as it leaves your hand, it will start turning, dipping or rising.

To make a paper airplane fly straight, you have to bend and straighten the nose, the wings, the tail sections until, by trial and error, you've got it tracking straight. You may even need to perfect your throwing motion to assure that you release the airplane on a straight path. Once done, you can achieve amazing accuracy with a paper airplane.

Without this tuning process, you'd be expecting a lot to think a paper airplane would fly as accurately as a dart. Yet that's exactly what many bowhunters do when they expect a broadhead tipped hunting arrow to hit in the same place as their field point arrows without spending the time and effort to tune their bows, their arrows and their shooting form.

The same adjustments required to make the paper airplane fly like a dart are also required to make a hunting arrow fly true. Your throwing motion is the action of the bow — to deliver the airplane or arrow flying on a straight path. The tweaking you do to the airplane itself is the same as the tweaking you do to an arrow to assure that all the components are lined up perfectly. If you think about tuning in these terms, this complex task seems a lot more straightforward.

LOOKING AHEAD

You can breakdown tuning into two categories. The first is bow tuning — making the arrow come out of the bow on a straight path. The second category is arrow tuning — making sure the arrow doesn't steer offline after it leaves the bow. Both are necessary to assure accuracy with hunting arrows. In the coming chapters, I will unwrap the methods to achieve both of these goals.

The first step is to set the bow up the right way so you get off on the right foot. The next three chapters will deal with setup, and then I get into the tweaks required to bring everything together. Stick with me on the journey to accuracy; this isn't as hard as it may seem.

Chapter 22

THE NOCKING POINT

How and where you attach your arrow to the string will affect how easily your bow tunes and how accurately you shoot it. You can make this important connection a number of ways. I'll lay out your options here. To give some idea of what is to come, there are two general ways to set your nocking point; you can use a string nocking loop and hook your release aid to the loop, or you can place a nock set on the string above the arrow's nock and then attach your release aid below the arrow. Here are the pros and cons of both styles.

A string loop improves serving life and promotes better arrow flight.

First, I may as well come clean and expose my bias. I'm a brass nock set guy because I have never been comfortable with the extra second or two it takes me to snag a string nocking loop. To its credit, the loop improves serving life and top archery coaches insist it promotes better arrow flight and accuracy. You must decide if these benefits are worth an extra second or two during the moment of truth.

WHERE IT GOES

Attach your nocking system (whichever one you choose) so the top knot of the loop or the bottom edge of the nock set (I always use two nock sets) positions the top of the arrow's nock one-eighth to one-quarter inch above the center of the riser's cushion plunger hole. The cushion plunger hole is the one you used when you attached the rest to the bow. You will need a simple T-square and a good nock plier for

Use a set of nocking pliers and a T-square to adjust nock height. Ideally, the top of the nock should be one-eighth to one-quarter inch above center of the serving.

this step if you use a crimp-on nock set.

Now it is time to decide which nocking style you will use, but first, it is useful to understand the concept of down pressure.

DOWN PRESSURE AND HOW IT'S CREATED

Down pressure is the slight downward press of the arrow on the arrow rest during the draw and while at full draw. Whenever the center of your release aid is below the center of the shaft, the string goes across the arrow's nock at an angle and this applies downward pressure.

When the release is in line with the shaft, you eliminate downward pressure. The reason for this quick tutorial on down pressure will become clearer as you consider the various options available for nocking the arrow and the affect each has on arrow flight and hunting performance.

DO YOU NEED DOWN PRESSURE?

I often rely on the advice of noted archer and bowhunter Randy Ulmer. Randy believes that slight down pressure between the arrow and the rest is valuable when you are setting up a bow for situations in which you may have to draw and shoot quickly. The slight pressure keeps the arrow more firmly pressed against the rest, so it is less likely to bounce off during the draw.

Top-ranked 3-D shooter Allen Conner likes a little downward pressure on the rest for all his shooting. According to Conner, down pressure produces more consistent arrow flight because it forces every arrow to correct the same, even if there are slight variations in the arrows themselves. When the shaft is free-floating, it is also free to find its own center when released. Without the guidance you get from consistent contact between the arrow and the rest, slight variations from one shaft to the next will cause subtle differences in accuracy.

Those in favor of a system with no down pressure feel that it improves arrow flight because the shaft makes less contact with the rest as it speeds forward. Any inconsistencies, they feel, can be eliminated by focusing on your arrows and removing or fixing those shafts that may be slightly bent, crooked, damaged or different in spine. They do this through trial and error — by shooting them all and using only those that group well together.

Testing done by Steve Johnson using his shooting machines suggests Allen Conner has the best approach for the average bowhunter. Steve noticed that he can improve his consistency by increasing the amount of time his arrow shaft slides along (and is guided by) the rest.

If you plan to use a drop-away rest, then you should be looking for ways to produce some down pressure and then set the rest so that it drops just in time to clear the fletching. In this way, you will provide the maximum amount of guidance to help stabilize the arrow before it is on its own. Obviously, if the rest drops immediately after the release of the string, any arrow with down pressure will certainly dip.

What is interesting is the affect this dip has on rests that have very light upward spring pressure. S.G. Christian, maker of the Bodoodle rest line, makes a rest called the Game Dropper. It is not technically a drop-away rest, but because of the dip in the arrow right after release, the arrow actually slings the rest support arms down. Their momentum carries them down far enough that the arrow's fletching is past and out of the way before they bounce back up to their original position. Christian determined this phenomenon by watching super slow-motion video of arrows being released.

Regardless of the philosophy you adopt, there are several options available for attaching the arrow to the string, and each has tradeoffs. And you thought this decision was a simple one. Fortunately, there are simple options but it is fun to

When the release is in line with the shaft at full draw, you eliminate downward pressure. How you nock your arrow can make a difference in arrow flight.

explore all the reasons why each option works or doesn't work.

CRIMP-ON NOCK SETS ABOVE THE ARROW

Most archery hunters have had at least some experience with standard crimp-on nock sets. The typical setup includes two brass nock sets crimped onto the string above the nock. Below the nock, you place a rubber donut sometimes called an "eliminator button" to cushion the nock from the release aid. And below the eliminator button you attach the jaws of your release aid.

You should also over-wrap the serving where the release contacts it using some kind of protective layer. I've used strand material from a spent Fast Flight string in the past, and it works just fine. You can also use a small diameter serving material that fits neatly down into and between the wraps of your string's primary serving.

Pros and cons: With the brass nock set option, the release head is placed well below the centerline of the arrow and presses firmly into the bottom of the nock. This creates maximum downward pressure on the rest. For this reason, it is not the method of choice for most archers using a drop-away rest.

Pictured is a setup using brass nock sets and a rubber cushion that goes between the arrow and the release aid. The author also recommends adding an overwrap that goes on the serving in the area where the release contacts it to extend the life of the serving.

There is another possible problem related to this method of setting up a string. I've had a number of bows through the years where the shaft's nock wanted to slide down the string, as the arrow was moving forward. This is related to the geometry of the bow. When the arrow is nocked well above the physical center of the string and the release is attached closer to the center (as it is in this case), you create a situation where the arrow's nock tries to slide down the string during the shot.

A rubber eliminator button will control this movement to a degree but there is still a problem with consistency when the button wears out and begins to lose its tight grip on the string. This problem is made worse by today's short bows that have acute string angles at full draw.

If, each time you place an arrow on the string, you have to slide the rubber button up to snug it against the nock you should sense a red flag waving. This should tell you right away that the nock slid down the string (pushing the button down) as the string sped forward. You are better off using a different system — one that controls the nock of the arrow better and eliminates this variable.

Crimp-on nock sets and a rubber eliminator button are a relatively heavy combination. Adding weight to the center of your string decreases your bow's efficiency slightly and results in reduced arrow speed. The difference between this system and other options might be as much as five feet per second.

But, there are also advantages to using brass nock sets. As I said, I use them, so there has to be something good to be gained. First, this method of nocking the arrow creates the least distraction when it comes time to hook up the release during the moment of truth. It is easier to grab the string anywhere with the release jaws and slide the release up the string than to try to snag a small loop. I can do it easily without ever taking my eyes off the approaching animal.

Second, this system is much faster for me. I can save at least two seconds when connecting my release by using this system. The speed of hookup is why I stopped using the string loop after just one season of hunting. I loved them for every other reason, but I felt that when things were happening fast, I was likely to fumble the connection with the loop and that would eventually cost me a shot at a good buck.

Perfecting the setup: Use two nock sets stacked above the arrow and crimped tightly to make sure they don't slide. However, you can get by with just one if

To create downward pressure, the bottom of the nock sets or the bottom of the top knot of a nocking loop should be roughly one-eighth to one-quarter inch above the center of the riser's cushion plunger hole.

you are shooting a bow with a draw weight below 50 pounds. Initially, set the bottom nock set so its lower edge is roughly one-eighth inch above the center of the cushion plunger hole. For bows that are less than 35 inches long, consider raising it another one eighth-inch to one quarter-inch above center to account for the sharper string angle.

CRIMP-ON NOCK SETS ABOVE AND BELOW THE ARROW

Another nocking method requires that you attach one crimp-on nock set above the arrow's nock and one below. Then you attach your release aid under the bottom one. You need plenty of spacing (especially with a short bow) so that the nock is not pinched tightly between the nock sets at full draw. I still see some bowhunters using this method of nocking the arrow, but for the most part it lost favor in the late '80s as bows became increasingly shorter and the gap between the nock sets grew. I don't see any reason to bring it back.

Pros and cons: This method of nocking an arrow introduces too many variables for my tastes. Primarily, the gap between the nock sets must be perfect and then closely monitored to assure it doesn't change.

THE CENTERED STRING LOOP

The centered string loop is the conventional loop that you see on most bowhunters' bows. The cord is tied above and below the arrow's nock, and the knots are snug to the arrow. When properly tied, you don't need to do anything else to lock the loop or the arrow in place. By properly tied, I mean you have to melt a decent sized ball at each end of the cord so that it won't pull through even when using heavy poundage.

Use specialized loop cord that you buy from an archery dealer or mail order shop. This specialized cord material is stiff enough to hold its shape making hook-ups with the release easier, and it won't stretch nearly as much as others I've tried.

In Chapter 4 I went into detail related to tying string nocking loops. If you didn't soak that up the first time, I suggest you go back and re-read that section.

Pros and cons: Of all the nocking systems, the simple loop has become the most recommended by top archers and archery coaches. I spoke with PSE shooting coach and instructor, George Chapman, about nocking systems. "If you've

Use only specialized string loop cord for your sting loops. Refer to Chapter 4 for an in-depth guide to string loop tying.

looked at as much slow motion video and instructed as many top archers as I have, you would never shoot anything but a string loop," he said. "It does everything well."

First, because the loop pulls equally above and below the arrow, it delivers the string's force uniformly to the shaft. There is no downward flex in the shaft that would create off-center loading upon release. Also, there is no fear that the nock will come off the string if you have to let down from full draw when game is near.

Second, the loop significantly reduces the likelihood of string serving failure because the release head never contacts the serving. It is easy to replace the loop as often as you like, whereas it is much

Being able to hook up your release quickly is critical when game approaches.

more difficult to reserve a string. Third, a simple loop is much lighter than most other options, so the loop doesn't rob your arrow of speed.

On the downside, some bowhunters (me) find it more difficult to load the release using a loop than when going straight to the string.

Using a loop once required that you give up at least a half inch of draw length and the arrow speed/kinetic energy that goes with it. Plus, there was always the hassle of having to adjust the bow appropriately to adjust for the difference in your anchor point (reduce the draw length). Today's specialized string loop release aids have short "noses" (the trigger is close to the jaw or jaws) so you no longer have to give up draw length to shoot a loop.

Perfecting the setup: In Chapter 4, you'll see the proper method for tying a loop on the string. Make a special point to reverse the knots on either side of the nock so you don't introduce a twisting action in the string. Start with the bottom of the upper knot roughly one eighth-inch above the center of the cushion plunger hole and work from there.

METAL D LOOPS

There are also metal D loops on the market that serve the same purpose as the cord loop. The metal loops are easier to attach than a cord loop and are obviously more durable (they are made of metal). However, they are also slightly heavier and have parts that have the potential of coming loose. The tradeoff between D loops and cord loops is not great — to each his own.

THE UNCENTERED STRING LOOP

Here is where we start to get into creative thinking. There are a number of ways that you can use a string loop and still create downward pressure on the arrow rest. Chuck Kidney, with Tiger Tuff arrow rests, suggests placing a nock set or tying on a nock point above the arrow and then tying both knots of the loop just below the arrow's nock. Slide both knots together and attach your release to the loop. This produces the characteristics of a rope release (releases that have ropes instead of jaws) with the quickness and security of attaching to a loop.

Kidney recommends this method for short bows when using conventional, launcher-style arrow rests and when shooting single-cam bows that have excessive nock travel. This is also Allen Conner's preferred setup for 3-D shooting (for hunting, he still attaches his release to the string under the arrow).

Randy Ulmer takes a different approach when he wants to achieve a slightly below center loop. Randy moves the lower knot downward by serving in a quarter-inch spacer between the loop's lower knot and the arrow's nock. The nock still contacts the upper knot directly. With Randy's system, the loop is held wide making it easier to get the release loaded. That's an important point to consider.

Pros and cons: The lower loop is a good choice for bowhunters who want to assure that they have some downward pressure on their arrow rest but still want all the other advantages of a string loop. The method Randy Ulmer advocates is ideal for bowhunters, providing down pressure and a wide loop for easy hookup.

Metal D-loops are easy to set up and are extremely durable however they are heavier than a string loop and have parts that could eventually come loose. Both string loops and metal D-loops have their own benefits.

SUMMARY

You can't go wrong with the standard string nocking loop, and you will be plenty accurate enough for hunting when using two brass nock sets above the arrow. Both systems will produce good results. However, each has its pros and cons. While the brass nock sets permit you to attach your release quickly to the string, the nocking loop reduces string wear and top coaches say it is more accurate. If you suspect you will need to shoot fast occasionally, the loop will be more precarious. Try them both. That is the fun of bowhunting; you can experiment until you come up with the perfect system for your shooting and hunting style.

LOOKING AHEAD

Now that we know where and how to attach the arrow to the string, we need to move on to setting up and adjusting the arrow rest. Positioning the arrow is key to easy tuning, so this next chapter is required reading.

Chapter 23

POSITIONING THE REST

Y ou must first adjust your rest up, down, in and out to properly position the arrow for a straight-line launch. There are several devices on the market that can help you determine the starting point, and they are all very useful, but you can also get very close simply by eyeballing the arrow as it lays across the rest.

HORIZONTAL ADJUSTMENT

This is the in and out part of the adjustment. When releasing the string with a release aid, adjust the rest until the arrow is directly in line with the forward thrust of the string. That sounds simple in principle, but requires a little thought to pull off. My approach is easy enough to understand and will get you very close.

Adjust the rest side to side until the shaft lines up exactly with the forward thrust of the string.

Stand the bow on its bottom cam with the arrow on the string, pointing away from you. Now, look down on the bow from above. When the rest is properly adjusted, the shaft should come straight out the front of the bow. You may need to lean the bow out in front of you holding one end of the top axle with your left index finger and the other with your right index finger to assure that the bow is square to your line of sight. If it appears that the arrow is pointing to one side or the other, you can easily move the rest in and out following the directions that came with the rest or through simple common sense.

If you have a stabilizer on the bow, the task of adjusting the center shot (the horizontal position of the arrow) is easier. When looking down on the rested arrow, the shaft should be parallel to the stabilizer when properly adjusted for horizontal position. I'm not saying it will run right down the center of the stabilizer because the stabilizer hole may be slightly offset, but it should be roughly parallel. If the stabilizer test doesn't agree with the simple arm's length sighting test, throw out the stabilizer test because there is no guarantee the manufacturer installed the stabilizer hole perfectly square to the riser.

This should be a great starting point for the horizontal position of the arrow when you begin tuning.

VERTICAL ADJUSTMENTS

Once again, you can easily make your vertical adjustments using just your eyes. Your goal is to move the rest up or down until the arrow is roughly perpendicular to the string. That means that where the arrow meets the string you should see a 90-degree angle. Of course, you could test the vertical position using a square, but your eyes (plus a little planning) will get you close enough. Here's how it works.

Adjust the rest up and down until the arrow goes across the center of the cushion plunger hole.

When we put the nock point on the string, we placed it a certain distance above the center of the cushion plunger hole (the hole your rest attaches to). You used a T-square to achieve this positioning. That distance wasn't arbitrary. The distance above the center of the cushion plunger hole is roughly half the width of your arrow nock. So now, if you simply raise or lower the rest until the arrow lies exactly in the center of the cushion plunger hole, you should be very close to the recommended starting point. When using fall-away rests, be sure your rest arms are in the upward position as if you were at full draw.

Sounds like a lot of garble, but the application is simple. While holding the bow so that the cushion plunger hole is at your eye level, move the rest up or down until the center of the arrow passes across the center of the plunger hole. Done.

ADJUSTING THE TIMING OF A DROP-AWAY REST

Most drop-away rests come with a pretty good set of instructions, but if yours doesn't, you can achieve a good starting point by shortening or lengthening the

Most drop-away rests have a setscrew that allows you to shorten or lengthen the cord that attaches to the downward moving buss cable. When adusting your drop-away rest, you want the rest to achieve its full height two to three inches prior to hitting your anchor point and full draw.

cord (or other mechanism that raises the rest) so that the rest has attained its full height when the string is still two to three inches short of full draw. That will allow the rest to support and guide initial forward thrust of the arrow, but still drop away in time to avoid the fletchings.

LOOKING AHEAD

I have adjusted my rests the way I detailed in this chapter for many years and typically, the bows (if they produce good nock travel) will tune with few further adjustments. Often, they tune perfectly when set up this way. Regardless of whether you get a bullet hole with the first arrow, this is a good starting point. I'll get into the tuning process — the tweaks to assure great arrow flight — in Chapter 25 through Chapter 29.

However, before we get into the nitty gritty of making an arrow fly true, we must first get the sight on the bow and properly set so you know where the arrow is going. That is the subject of the next chapter.

Chapter 24

SETTING UP YOUR SIGHTING SYSTEM

Now that you have attached your rest, you can begin to think about shooting the bow. The next step is to install your sight. It is a very cut and dried process.

Start by attaching the sight to the bow. Next, loosen the screw that locks the horizontal adjustment of the sight head and place an arrow on the rest. Move the sight head in or out until the pins line up with both the string and the nocked arrow. Often, the pins will end up slightly to the left of the arrow, but start with everything lined up.

Since I center my round sight housing inside my peep sight, I like to set my sight so that the middle pin is right in the center of the housing. This looks the most natural to my eye. Then, I sight in the 20-yard pin by moving the entire housing up or down.

The only problem with this strategy occurs if you have a high anchor point such

After installing your sight, adjust it horizontally so the pins line up with the center of your rest and string. Once sighted in, your pins will typically fall just left of the string when holding the bow straight in front of you.

Move individual pins inside the sight body only if the pin gaps are incorrect. Otherwise, you can move the entire sight body to put your arrows back on the mark. Sighting in may take several days until you know you have the bow perfectly dialed in.

as up by your earlobe (mine is down by the corner of my jawbone). A high anchor point will force your sight pins downward and your primary vertical dovetail will likely run out of adjustment room before you get the pins low enough. When that happens you will need to move the pins down inside the housing.

SIGHTING IN

If you are hitting above the intended spot, move the pin up. Move it down if you are hitting below your intended spot. If you are hitting to the left of the spot, move the pin to the left. Move it to the right if you are hitting to the right of the spot.

Spread the project over several days; your form can change slightly from one day to the next, so you need to work the pins into the right place over time to get the best results. This has the affect of averaging your shots together. It may take five different practice sessions to get a bow sighted in perfectly.

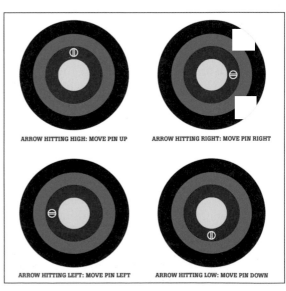

ARROW HITTING HIGH: MOVE PIN UP

ARROW HITTING RIGHT: MOVE PIN RIGHT

ARROW HITTING LEFT: MOVE PIN LEFT

ARROW HITTING LOW: MOVE PIN DOWN

CHOOSING THE ALIGNMENT SYSTEM

After getting your bow roughly sighted in, it is time to attach and tweak your rear sight. Without question, you need something to provide a second alignment reference when shooting your bow. Just as a rifle shooter would never consider shooting his favorite gun without a rear sight, your bow also needs a rear sight.

You have options. I am a big believer in using a large peep sight — I already explained why in Chapter 14. To go a step further, I will now tell you why I prefer peep sights in general. I feel a peep sight locks me into my anchor point and assures a consistently aligned sight picture better than other methods I have tried. Also, I am a sworn minimalist. I don't like to attach a lot of stuff to my bow. I live by the motto, "Keep It Simple Stupid." In fact, I could be the poster child for a national Keep It Simple Stupid campaign. So, that bias prevents me from using some of the other systems on the market. As I mentioned, however, you do have other options.

Several companies make systems that feature a conventional fiber optic pin sight body and an extension pointing rearward that serves as the rear sight. I have tried these and they definitely work, but they do add to the complexity and weight of the bow. On the upside, they eliminate the need for a peep sight and thus they increase your field of view and your visibility in low light.

Gang adjustable sights are the only choice, because once you have set the gaps between pins, all you have to do when you change your rest setting or nocking point is move the entire sight body horizontally or vertically to quickly re-sight the bow.

Large peep sights like G5 Outdoors' ⁵⁄₁₆-inch Meta Peep are growing in popularity. They promote a consistent reference point and larger sight picture.

A kisser button is another option. A kisser button is a small disk that attaches on the string at a point where it contacts your lips or touches the corner of your mouth at full draw. The kisser also serves to improve low light visibility and field of view.

I have hunted with only a kisser button on my string and it works great on short shots. If you practice often so that your anchor point and body positions are consistent, and limit yourself to shots of less than 30 yards, this system will work fine. However, I sometimes shoot past 30 yards and the kisser button doesn't cut it. In fact, a kisser button used without a peep is only slightly more accurate than shooting with no rear sight whatsoever.

Again, archery offers you the chance to experiment and personalize your equipment to match your exact style of shooting. My recommendations will serve as a great starting point, but you can take it from there. Unless you have a strong objection to peep sights, I would simply start with an inexpensive peep

There are sights available that actually allow you to shoot without a peep if focusing or aiming in low light is a problem. Hind Sight sights feature a rear reference aiming system, which offers a larger field of view. If you choose, you can use a peep sight with this system.

sight in the string. You can always change your system later.

Installing a peep sight: To keep your peep sight from rotating dramatically when you draw the bow, be sure to place it in the center of the string. When strings are made, the builder twists up two different bundles of fibers. You need to be able to separate these two bundles. Ideally, the string builder used two different color fibers so you can immediately identify the center. If not, finding it will be much more difficult, maybe impossible. You need to remove all tension from the string and see if you can determine the center by examining the way it looks and behaves right where it comes out of the end serving. This is a good reason to own a two-tone string.

After you put the peep in, take the bow out of the press, put an arrow on the string and draw it back. Through a process of small movements, line the peep up perfectly with your eye and your sight pins when you pull back to your most comfortable anchor point.

A kisser button is one option when setting up your bow. It provides a reference point of contact on your face while aiming at full draw to improve consistency. However, don't think you can eliminate your peep sight simply by using a kisser button.

Once you have everything lined up, serve the peep into place. I use a simple wrap using strand material from a worn out bowstring and tie it off the same way I tie off my center serving. It may not be fancy, but it is quick and simple and stays in place.

Shoot the bow several times to set the string before you start dealing with peep rotation. When the peep appears to be rotating the same every time, remove one end of the string (using the bow press again) and add twists (or half twists) until the peep comes back square to your eye every time you draw.

This process will take place over a few days as the string settles and stretches, but once it stabilizes, the peep will not move for months — possibly even years. I have a bow with a custom string on it (custom strings typically are pre-stretched, so they stabilize very quickly). The way the peep rotates has not changed for

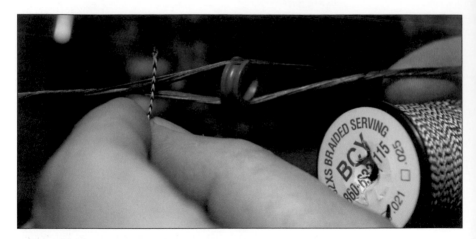

It's best to use a bowpress when installing a peep sight. To keep your peep from rotating, install it in the center of the string. Two-toned fibers make this job much easier.

three years, even though I shoot the bow for two solid months leading up to the hunting season.

LOOKING AHEAD

Now you should have your bow hitting the target more or less where you are aiming. It is time to address the bigger issue of arrow flight. You may get lucky and your bow will tune with the very first arrow. Sometimes that happens. However, you will likely have to make a few adjustments to your rest, nocking point and possibly to your bow's cam system to produce perfect arrow flight. That is our next challenge in our road to better bowhunting. Turn the page; Bow Tuning 101 starts with the next chapter.

Chapter 25

PAPER TUNING YOUR BOW

N othing instills confidence better than perfect arrow flight. I love watching an arrow zip through the cool fall air. It gives me the feeling I am soon going to be doing the same thing with a big deer in front of me.

Perfect flight means that the tail of the arrow follows the exact same course as the tip as the arrow speeds forward. The easiest way to test arrow flight is to shoot through paper. Keep it simple; cut a hole through a cardboard box then tape a piece of copier paper over the opening.

Paper tuning — stand about six feet away with the backstop far enough behind that the arrow is clear of the paper before hitting the backstop.

Before paper tuning your bow, be sure to have properly spined arrows and check to make sure your arrows don't have cracked nocks and ends. It's best to use new arrows when paper tuning, or at the minimum, replace the nocks.

Stand back six feet from the paper and shoot through it. Make sure that the arrow is clear of the paper before it hits the backstop. Use the same form you use when shooting at targets. In other words, don't punch the trigger or grip the bow differently when shooting through the paper. That will show up in your arrow flight. The ideal result is a nice clean hole with three thin tears radiating outward caused by the fletching.

If the arrow is coming out of the bow other than perfectly straight, the tail of the arrow will tear the paper up, down or to the side. That information is all you need to make adjustments to your bow or shooting form.

This isn't hard. There are only a few basic adjustments you will need to make. If they don't fix the problem, I will get into a few slightly more advanced techniques.

First, make sure that you are shoot-ing an arrow that is the proper stiffness for your bow. Consult the arrow manufacturer's selection charts. Varying stiffness can change arrow flight considerably.

Arrow straightness also has a huge affect on arrow flight. If the arrow or the nock is bent, the arrow will not fly well. Try to use new arrows when tuning to eliminate any problems related to the nock or shaft straightness. At the very least, replace your nocks to be sure that they are not dinged from target practice.

MAKING THE ADJUSTMENTS

Now you have shot your arrow through the paper. It is best to shoot three or four different arrows through the paper to make sure that you are not trying to fix a bad arrow by tweaking your bow. That never works. Once you are sure all the arrows are flying

Moving the nocking point up can eliminate some tail low tears and moving it down can eliminate some tail high tears.

the same (set aside any that aren't) it is time to work on the bow.

Tail high: If the arrow tears the paper tail high (the nock rips above the tips), you should move the nock point on your string down one eighth-inch and take another shot. The tear should get smaller or go away completely. If it doesn't, you have a different problem and you should put your nock point back where it started (presumably one eighth-inch above the center of the cushion plunger hole).

Check your fletching. It can show signs of contact that will help diagnose your arrow flight problem.

If that doesn't fix the tear, your arrow fletchings may be contacting your arrow rest. If you are using a conventional rest that requires one fletching to pass through a gap (called a shoot-through rest), turn the nock so that one of the fletchings points straight at the middle of the gap when you nock an arrow. Experiment with various nock rotation positions to see if a slight tweak will change your arrow flight.

The easiest way to check for contact is to buy a spray can of foot powder at the grocery store, spray your fletchings liberally and take a shot. If you have contact, you should see where the rest has brushed the powder off one or two fletchings. Turn the nock slightly until you eliminate this contact.

If you have a persistent contact problem, you have two choices: a different rest or different fletchings. I'll offer more about both of these options later. Also, in the next section, I will offer a more advanced method to address a tail high tear if you can't eliminate it by making these simple adjustments.

Tail low: If the arrow tears the paper tail low, raise the nocking point one eighth-inch and shoot again. The tear should get smaller or go away. If it doesn't, chances are you are experiencing a cam-timing problem — more about that in the next section.

Tail right: If the arrow tears the paper tail right, move the rest to the left.

PERFECT BULLET HOLE   HIGH TEAR   RIGHT TEAR

LOW TEAR   LEFT TEAR

Pictured are examples of paper tears. If both horizontal and vertical tears are present, adjust for the vertical tear first.

Adjustments to your rest can include moving it side to side to eliminate tail right and tail left tears.

You may also find, with certain kinds of rests, that actually moving the rest to the right will improve this tear. Most rests are easy to move to the left or right, so experiment freely to find the best position.

Tail right tears are also common when the cam or cams of the bow lean during the draw and shot. This happens because the forces acting on the limb tips aren't balanced throughout the shot on most bows, causing the limb tips to twist slightly. The string moves to the left as you draw it back and then moves back right when you release. The arrow comes out tail right (for a right-handed shooter).

If you can't eliminate a tail right tear no matter what you do (including testing for fletching contact), a few advanced repairs (possibly even a new set of limbs) may fix this problem, but those adjustments are beyond the scope of this chapter. Consider taking the bow to a good archery pro for help at this point.

Don't give up yet, you may find that your tail right tear will improve with a different arrow having a slightly different stiffness that works better with the sideways movement of the bowstring. I'll come back to this later.

Tail left: If the arrow is tearing tail left move the rest to the right and again experiment quickly to see if moving it to the left will produce an improvement instead. A tail left paper tear is uncommon for a right-handed shooter and may signify incorrect arrow stiffness. Try a different arrow if this problem persists.

If you run into a combination of tears, such as one high and to the right, fix the vertical portion of the tear first and then work on the horizontal portion. In other words, for a high right tear, initially treat it as a tail high tear.

IF THE ADJUSTMENTS DON'T FIX THE PROBLEM

I like to see any new bow tune straight out of the box using only the basic adjustments described in Chapter 22 and Chapter 23. And many will. However, at times you will have to look deeper for the solution.

If you can't fix tail low tears, the only reasonable explanation is cam timing or design. Check with your bow manufacturer or local pro shop to find out how to tune your cam for better arrow flight.

Cam timing: Cam timing describes the rotation of the cam before you draw the string. If the timing is too far off, the bow will shoot arrows that tear the paper tail high or tail low. Timing is important on single and hybrid cam bows, but is critical when tuning a two-cam bow.

If you suspect your cams are out of time, have someone watch your cams as you draw the bow for inconsistencies in their rotations.

Three Tricks To Beat Fletching Contact

As you mingle with the other shooters at the neighborhood archery range, take a look at their fletchings. Most of the arrows you see in quivers will have scuff marks and damage caused by contact with the rest. Next to target panic, this sort of contact is one of archery's biggest plagues. Fletching-to-rest contact is the biggest challenge when tuning a bow; use any method you can to eliminate it. I detailed this subject at some length above, but because it is such an important part of arrow tuning, I am going to summarize the steps in this short sidebar.

A drop-away rest will eliminate contact for better arrow flight, permitting more aggressive helical fletching with small carbon arrows.

Try a Drop-Away Rest: The best way to eliminate fletching contact with the rest is to eliminate the rest. The only way you can do that is by employing a drop-away rest — one that clears the path of the fletching as soon as the string is released. If you don't want to buy a drop-away rest, you have two other options that might work.

Try Feather Fletching: When a plastic vane contacts the rest it is prone to kick the tail of the arrow significantly offline. If you have been shooting plastic vanes and are having trouble getting rid of contact with the rest, feather fletching will not eliminate the contact but it will reduce the affects. Feathers flatten at the point of contact

and soften the affect, reducing the amount the arrow kicks offline.

Change Fletching Length and Offset: You can sometimes eliminate contact by switching to shorter fletchings. In other cases, long fletchings with a low profile will improve flight. You might also consider adjusting the amount of helical offset applied to your fletchings. With all this experimentation, is it any wonder I recommend that you learn to build your own arrows? True Flight Arrow Company has done years of testing to determine the best arrow components. They recommend eight degrees of helical offset. But you may do better with more or slightly less.

Short fletching may reduce contact problems. The short, high-profile designs popular today also are recommended for bowhunting.

If the cams of a two-cam bow are not properly synchronized (one cam gets to its full draw position slightly before the other), the bow will never shoot properly. Timing a two-cam bow is not particularly hard, but it does require a bow press. So if you suspect your cams are not correctly timed (have someone watch them as you draw the bow), you may want to take it to a pro shop. Pay attention to how the technician tests and fixes the problem and you should be able to easily monitor and fix the timing yourself in the future.

Single-cam and hybrid-cam bows tend to be more forgiving of harness stretch than two-cam bows, but they still have a rotational position where they work best. The length of the control cable positions the single-cam or the master cam,

Feather fletching can reduce the affects of contact and improve arrow flight.

in the case of the hybrid system. The manufacturer may have inscribed the correct cam rotation markings on the cams themselves. If so, compare these markings to the diagram in your owner's manual to be sure your bow is set up to operate in its sweet spot. If you don't have the owner's manual, call the customer service number for the company that made your bow.

If you have a persistent tail low tear, the only reasonable culprit is cam design or cam timing. Contact the manufacturer or find a good Internet forum where you can learn more about tweaking your bow's cam rotation to produce better nock travel and better arrow flight.

A new rest: If you have persistent fletching contact problems and you can't keep from scuffing foot powder off your fletchings simply by rotating the nock, you have two options: a new rest or different fletchings. Drop-away arrow rests minimize or eliminate fletching contact and are a good choice. Also, surprisingly, rests that produce maximum contact (contact on all sides of the shaft) such as the Whisker Biscuit, can also eliminate poor arrow flight that occurs when only one fletching contacts the rest and kicks the arrow to the side. If you choose the Whisker Biscuit, be sure to use short, stiff vanes such as the Bohning Blazer to reduce fletching damage.

Different fletching: Changing fletching can have a big affect on arrow flight if you are trying to eliminate persistent contact. Not only are there many styles of vanes (and many lengths), but you can also experiment with feather fletching. Many bowhunters are finding excellent accuracy with short, stiff, high-profile vanes that are only two to three inches long.

A different arrow: If you hit a wall in your tuning and can't figure out what to do next, consider experimenting with arrows of a different stiffness. You can accomplish this by buying (it would be better if you can just try a few different ones at the pro shop) a few new arrows or attaching heavier or lighter points to the front of your existing arrows. Perfect arrow flight may require a combination of the two.

Bow tuning is not overly complex if you follow this step-by-step process of elimination. The result — a perfect arrow sizzling like a bullet through the cool, still fall air — definitely justifies the time and head scratching required.

LOOKING AHEAD

OK, we have jumped head first into the tuning process. I hope you now have a bow shooting perfect arrows. If not, there is still hope, because in the next four chapters, I am going to go even deeper into this subject. If, after reading the next three chapters, you don't have a tuned bow, you may own a lemon — an untuneable bow. I have saved that subject until the end of this section. I have assumed in the chapter you have just finished that you shot a release aid. In the next chapter, I will offer a tuning method for finger shooters. If you don't release the string with your fingers (and never will) you can jump right past the next few pages.

Chapter 26

BARE SHAFT TUNING

B ow tuning can sometimes leave even advanced finger shooters scratching their heads. That is because the fingers introduce another variable to the equation that release aid shooters don't have to deal with; it is called paradox.

Paradox is the side-to-side flexing of the arrow as it accelerates forward from the bow of a finger shooter. This is caused by the way the string slips off the fingers. Regardless of how good you become at letting the string slip smoothly away, it will always move sideways when it clears your fingertips. With a good, trained release, it will not move much, but with a rough, strumming, plucking release, it will move dramatically.

When the string moves sideways, it causes the tail of the arrow (the nock is still attached to the string) to move with it. This causes the arrow to flex just as it is starting forward. The first flex is for the nock to move outward. The shaft will rebound even before it leaves the bow and the nock will move back toward the bow. This causes the center of the arrow to move slightly away from the bow. And then the final flex occurs as the nock moves back away from the bow.

In order for all this flexing to occur without the arrow hitting the bow, you need the exact arrow stiffness that complements your draw weight, arrow length and release style. With the correct stiffness, the arrow will actually flex around the bow and not touch it, producing good arrow flight.

The manufacturer's arrow selection charts will get you close, but the final tweaking will occur only after you engage in the hands-on tuning I will describe next.

THE METHOD

For years, finger shooters have shot unfletched (bare) shafts in order to determine what corrections to make to their bow and arrow setups when tuning. Bare

Bare Shaft Tuning Tips

High Hit: Move the nock point down, check fletching contact and cam wheel timing.

Right Hit: Try a more flexible shaft, increase point weight or turn up your bow poundage. You may also tweak the rest position slightly left or right.

ARROW HITTING HIGH

ARROW HITTING RIGHT

ARROW HITTING LEFT

ARROW HITTING LOW

Left Hit: Try a stiffer shaft, a lighter point or reduce your draw weight. You can also reduce the length of your arrow.

Low Hit: Check cam timing or move your nock point up.

shaft tuning is a proven, systematic method to achieve the best possible arrow flight. It is often impossible for a finger shooter to achieve a perfect bullet hole through paper the way a release aid shooter often can. So, rather than get frustrated trying to achieve the impossible, they focus on downrange performance. If the arrows are flying true at 20 yards, everything is good.

First, shoot a group of arrows into the target at a distance of 20 yards using fletched (not bare) shafts. Mark the center of the group. Next, from the same distance, shoot a group using bare shafts and mark this center. If both groups have essentially the same center, your system is tuned. However, if the bare shafts plane off-line, you'll have to make corrections.

Here is a general guideline to the proper corrections when your bare shaft groups

What Bare Shaft Tuning Can Teach Release Aid Shooters

I used to paper tune all my bows using a bare shaft even though I was releasing the string with fingers. I did this for two reasons. First, it eliminated all concern about fletching contact. I could then focus on rest and nock position. After I had the bare shaft flying perfectly, I would then switch back to fletched shafts to see if I was still getting a bullet hole. If I wasn't, I knew that fletching contact was the culprit.

This process of elimination made tuning more precise. With the advent of drop-away rests, I stopped tuning this way, but it still makes a lot of sense. Even with drop-away rests and full capture rests, you can learn immediately if there is any kind of disturbance to the arrow from the bristles of the capture rest or from a launcher that drops too slowly when shooting a drop-away rest.

If you shoot a bare shaft through paper, you can also learn important information about your shooting form. Here are a few examples of what I mean.

Hand position is key to consistent accuracy. Pay close attention to how you hold the bow and work out a system that promotes a consistent grip.

Bow Hand Position: Shooting a bare shaft through paper at a range of three yards provides immediate and extremely critical feedback on the quality of your grip. Several years ago, I was helping a buddy tune his new bow. He's left-handed, and for some reason, we simply could not eliminate a hard left paper tear. I was perplexed. In an effort to determine if it was some kind of weird contact problem, we removed the fletching from one of his shafts and shot it through the paper. It slashed even more wildly to the left.

The light bulb came on in my head. I took my buddy's left-handed bow and shot it right-handed. The arrow made a perfect bullet hole on the first shot! Even though my friend is an accomplished archer, I immediately knew he was holding the bow wrong. He was trying to shoot the new bow using the same hand position he'd used on his old bow. By experimenting with a couple of minor grip changes, my friend was soon making a perfect bullet hole. He found that by simply applying a little more thumb pressure to the side of the grip he could solve the problem with no discomfort or loss of accuracy.

This brings up an important point. I've tuned many different bow styles through the years. Most of them required slight grip changes to make them tune perfectly. That is one reason why some bowhunters get stuck on one bow brand — their bow hands have learned to seek the proper no-torque position automatically on familiar grips. The quickest way to determine if your bow hand position is faulty is to shoot a bare shaft through paper and experiment with different grips.

Other Form Flaws: In my own shooting, I've been able to isolate various departures from correct form that were destroying arrow flight and making good accuracy literally a hit and miss deal. When you're shooting fast arrows, 260 fps or faster, it becomes more difficult to group exposed blade broadheads consistently beyond 25 yards. If you hurry the release, or get a little tense, the arrow will veer offline.

The trend is toward smaller heads to solve this problem and it is an effective solution, but this is only a Band-Aid. It is better to eliminate the root cause of such shooting problems: grip tension, hand position and a rough release. Shooting a bare shaft through paper gives you the feedback you need to become a better archer.

If your bare shaft groups are higher than your fletched arrow group, move your nocking point higher. If the bare shaft group is lower, move your nocking point lower.

are different from your fletched shaft groups. If the bare shaft group is to the left, try a more flexible shaft, increased point weight or turn up your bow poundage. You may also tweak the rest position slightly left or right. After doing so, you will need to establish a new baseline by shooting another group with your fletched arrows.

If the bare shaft group is below the fletched shaft group, move the nock point down, check fletching contact with the rest by spraying the fletching with aerosol foot powder and check wheel timing.

If the bare shaft group is to the right, try a stiffer shaft, a lighter point or reduce your draw weight. You can also reduce the length of your arrow slightly (one half-inch at a time, if you have the room), because shortening the arrow also serves to make it act stiffer. Again, you can experiment with the left and right rest position, but you will have to re-establish your baseline group by shooting your fletched arrows again.

If the bare shaft group hits higher than the fletched shaft group, check wheel timing or move your nock point up.

I have seen finger shooters who were so good at this they could literally hit a two-inch bull's-eye with both fletched and unfletched arrows from the same bow. However, you may never reach this level of perfection. Get as close as you can and in time, your shooting form may smooth out and your arrow flight will improve.

LOOKING AHEAD

In the last two chapters, I have gone into the techniques for tuning a bow when you use a mechanical release and when you release with fingers. I hope you understand the process better now and are ready to tackle the task. Next, I'm going to get into a bit more detail about how to fine-tune the various cam styles on the market. I have already written at some length about setting cam timing for a two-cam bow, so I will skip over that and get right into the inner workings of the hybrid and single-cam models.

Chapter 27

SPECIAL TUNING TIPS FOR HYBRID-CAM BOWS

Y ou will encounter a common theme when studying the methods for tuning both hybrid- and single-cam bows: there is not much you can do if the cams aren't designed well. In other words, the vertical portion of the nock travel depends on the design of the cams. If they are well designed, the nock travel will be more or less level and your bow should tune relatively easily. If they are not well designed, you will have a very hard, or impossible, time tuning your bow.

HYBRID CAMS MUST BE TIMED

As mentioned in Chapter 6, a hybrid-cam system reduces the affects of power cable (buss cable) stretch because the bow's other harness (the control cable) ties both the top and bottom cams together so neither can turn without turning the other — effectively keeping them synchronized.

If the power cable stretches without the control cable stretching, nothing much happens other than a slight change in draw length. However, if the control cable stretches, the cams will change timing very slightly. When the control cable stretches, the bottom cam and top cam rotate different amounts because the power cable anchors the bottom cam while the top cam is not anchored (merely slaved to the bottom).

Simplifying, the last paragraph is just a long-winded way of saying that hybrid cams can go out of time, but they are much less sensitive to changes in harness length than a two-cam bow. Hybrid systems are also less sensitive to harness stretch, because there is not much load on the control cable, so it is very unlikely to stretch past its initial break-in period.

I recently spoke with several representatives from bow manufacturers that offer hybrid-cam bows. They all agreed that a hybrid cam must remain in time if the bow is to shoot the way it was designed. Again, remember it is rare to have significant timing issues with hybrid-cam bows. The number one cause of timing problems is the settling of the harnesses in the tracks, and that generally occurs from the time the bow is built until it finds it way onto the rack at the archery shop.

The number one reason hybrid cams get out of time is due to the settling of the harnesses in the cams' tracks.

You time a hybrid-cam bow the same way you time a two-cam bow except there is just one harness (the control cable) to adjust. It is the one that ties the two cams together. You can shorten it by adding twists and lengthen it by removing twists. More than likely, you won't have to lengthen it, because stretch is the primary reason a hybrid cam bow slips out of time.

To determine if your hybrid-cam system is properly synchronized, watch the harness tracks just as you do with a two-cam bow. The harnesses should both hit their stops at the same time when you get to full draw.

While hybrid-cam bows are certainly more forgiving of harness stretch than two-cam bows, they may still require a bit of vigilance shortly after you buy the bow (or replace the cables) to assure that the cams are hitting full draw at the same time.

LOOKING AHEAD

We have looked at two-cam bows and now hybrid-cam bows. Next, I will get into special tuning tips for single-cam bows. They are just as user-friendly as hybrid-cam bows, but like the hybrids, they also require a bit of attention to assure that they shoot as accurately as possible.

Chapter 28

SPECIAL TUNING TIPS FOR SINGLE-CAM BOWS

Single-cam bows became popular because they eliminated concerns about cam timing. Aggressive two-cam bows will go out of time if one harness stretches more than the other. This makes tuning impossible until the problem is fixed. While there is more information available now on checking and setting cam timing on two-cam bows — and better synthetics that don't stretch as easily — the majority of bowhunters still want the speed without the hassle. Consequently, single-cam bows (and hybrid-cam bows) now dominate the market.

In little more than a decade, single-cam bows have gone from being a little-heralded technology footnote to one of the most significant archery inventions since the compound bow. The reason is simple: they solve a problem. Since nearly everyone is now shooting single-cam bows, it's time to take a look at the current state-of-the-art and the best ways to get these bows to shoot their best.

Mathews' Solocam is one of the greatest archery inventions of all time.

Although single-cam and two-cam bows tune much the same, some single-cam bows require a slightly higher nock point.

THINGS TO CONSIDER

Level nock travel: The first single-cam bows were difficult to tune because the nock took the scenic route from full draw to its pre-draw position. It was difficult to produce perfect arrow flight. However, in the last few years, tremendous research and development has brought us level nock travel on most single-cam bows. It is debatable whether perfectly level nock travel is required for good accuracy, but intuitively it makes sense. I want it and you should too. The less the nock wavers while moving forward, the more stable the arrow and better the arrow flight.

With the current design options available, you can (and should) demand a single-cam bow that produces level nock travel. More than likely, it will be a bow that has a dedicated cam size. In other words, it won't use modules. There are exceptions, but in general, the modular single-cam bows give up perfect nock travel in exchange for draw length flexibility. Just to be safe, be sure to test tune any bow before you buy it. Don't assume it will tune for you.

Equal tiller: The first single-cam bows also exhibited uneven tiller measurements (when measured from the back of the limb near the pocket to the string) because the idler wheel was much smaller than the cam. However, the current design scheme used in single-cam bows produces equal tiller. These bows are easier to keep adjusted, since you don't have to factor in an offset every time you set them up. Single-cam bows can be made to shoot very well even if they don't have an equal tiller setting, but given the choice, keep things simple by opting for one that's designed for equal tiller.

You can also determine and set tiller on a single-cam bow by running a piece of thread or serving material from the top axle to the bottom axle and then measuring the distance between the back of the limbs to this line. Using this method of measuring tiller, you won't be influenced by the size of the cam or idler wheel.

SETUP CHANGES

Single-cam bows and two-cam bows tune much the same, but with a few small differences. I spoke with Allan Smith, a former engineer at PSE, Parker's Johnny Grace, and Derek Phillips, shooting staff coordinator for Mathews, about any special tuning requirements of a single-cam bow. Here are their insights.

Initial nock point: Grace recommends an initial nock point setting that is one-eighth inch higher for a single-cam bow than a two-cam bow. Grace believes this is due to the way single-cam bows move on release.

Tiller setting: "We like to see people shoot their bows with both limbs bottomed or very close to being bottomed," said Phillips. "This is the best position for optimum brace height, limb stress and performance. If you do back your limbs out, maintain an equal tiller setting between the top and bottom limbs. Single-cam bows are designed to be shot with an equal tiller setting."

Keep in mind that not all single-cam bows have equal measurement when the limbs are bottomed due to small idler wheels. To assure that you are shooting the bow with equal limb flex (the real goal), first bottom both limbs and then back them off equally until you reach the desired draw weight.

Monitor string stretch: Both Allan Smith and Derek Phillips recommended measuring your nock point precisely after tuning the bow and sighting it in. Compare it to a fixed location, such as the cushion plunger hole, by using a calibrated T-square. Single-cam bows with a string that doesn't terminate at the idler wheel are more susceptible to stretch. The nock point is only one-quarter of the way up from one end of the string, which means it will move down in relation to the bow's plunger hole when the entire string stretches. This relative movement impacts the bow's tuning and accuracy, as well as draw length and peak draw weight.

Even though today's synthetics are much more resistant to stretch, it still pays to check your bow often to make sure the string hasn't gotten longer. When it does, twist both sides equally, not just the one where the nock point is attached.

By using a T-square, you can measure your nocking point and see if the string has stretched. When you first get your bow, take notes for later reference.

A stiffer arrow: Grace said the biggest problem they find when dealing with customer complaints about poor arrow flight is shaft stiffness. "This problem usually appears as an up or down tear through paper when tuning," he said. "Easton could almost put in a separate category for single-cam bows in their arrow selection guide, because we've seen that they are more sensitive to stiffness than two-cam bows. Maybe it's because they are so aggressive, but modern, single-cam bows almost always require stiffer shafts — at least one shaft size up from what's shown on the chart."

CAM ROTATION

To perform best, the cam must be in the proper rotation before you start to draw your bow. This will assure that it produces the very best speed and efficiency, nock travel and reaches the bow's designated draw length. If the cam is under-rotated, the cam will look like the string is too short, like the string has pulled the cam around too far.

If you find this situation, put a few twists in the control cable. The control cable is the one that goes from the cam directly to the axle on the other limb tip (not the one that either attaches to the idler wheel or wraps around the idler wheel and then attaches to the bottom cam again). If the cam is over-rotated, (which is the normal case resulting from string stretch) put twists in the string equally on both sides.

Of course, the next question is this: how do I know what the cam rotation is supposed to be? You can find it in two places. First, take special note of the rotation of the cam when the bow is new — before the string and cable break in. Make a few measurements and take a few notes. Next, call the customer service number for the company that made your bow or look in the owner's manual to see if they have shown an illustration of the correct rotation there.

Regardless of how you find it, this is the position you want to come back to when the string or control cables stretch, or when you replace the string or cable.

Single-cam bows are designed to be easier to tune, but you still have to tune them. You'll need to use the same basic adjustments outlined in the other chapters on tuning to eliminate paper tears, but if you start by realizing that single-cam bows have their own personality, it is more likely that you'll be good to go from the very first arrow.

LOOKING AHEAD

Now that we have dug into all the fine points of tuning a bow, and you have a good handle on how to make your bow shoot a perfect arrow, I'm sure you will be excited to learn that some bows can't be tuned! Oh boy, now you tell me! The truth is, there were many bows back in the '90s that were untunable, but the number has gone down steadily since because bowhunters and manufacturers alike have learned more and demanded higher standards. In the next chapter, I'll get into the subject of untunable bows in more detail. I hope you don't own one.

Chapter 29

UNTUNABLE BOWS

I 've owned bows that were so bad that they were impossible to tune. I'm not talking about isolated cases either. I've owned a bunch of them. Such bows were very common in the 1990s and even as recently as the early 2000s. Everyone was making fast bows, but few knew how to make them correctly.

If a bow has good level nock travel, there is no reason that through testing different combinations of arrow sizes and rest styles, you can't enjoy repeatable accuracy on a day-to-day basis.

These bows were bad because the nock point on the string moved dramatically up, down or sideways during the shot. If a bow has level and straight nock travel, I can tune it every single time, and so can you. There is no problem eventually working out the combination of adjustments, arrow

Evaluating Cam Lean

As stated in Chapter 7, horizontal nock travel is generally the result of cam lean. The cam leans and takes the string with it on a sideways course.

Steve Johnson, who makes the Hooter Shooter shooting machine, has a systematic way to evaluate the cam lean on his personal bows using his shooting machine. Any pro shop that uses one of his Hooter Shooters (there are more than 200 nationwide) should be able to perform this same test. Johnson places a small pen laser against the cam to project a dot from the top cam to the bottom limb and from the bottom cam to the top limb both before the bow is drawn and again at full draw. In this way, he can tell how much the cam tilts and how much it changes when the machine draws the bow. He says his sweetest shooting bows have a change in laser dot movement of one half-inch, or less, for each cam.

Cam lean can be attributed to misaligned axle holes.

According to Johnson, the bows with the least amount of cam tilt right from the box have been target bows. More aggressive cams on hard shooting hunting bows load up more and this produces limb torque and cam lean. It is not fair to single out one bow model as bad, because they vary too much. You may test one bow that is bad and then grab an identical bow off the shelf next to it and find it tunes perfectly. In one case, the axle holes may be drilled slightly offline or one of the limb pockets may not be perfectly aligned with the riser. This is why you need to test tune every bow before you buy.

shaft and rest style that will produce a perfect bullet hole through paper. However, when nock travel is poor, the job becomes infinitely harder at best or impossible at worst. All the untunable bows I have encountered through the years were the result of poor nock travel.

I went into considerable detail in Chapter 7 about nock travel and the problems that occur when it is anything but straight back and straight forward. I'm not going to repeat that material here. It is simply enough to know that you will never tune some bows — no one can. If you fear that you have one of these bows, go back and read Chapter 7 again. If that doesn't help, I fear you are simply out of luck.

This subject touches a nerve with me. Poor quality is my pet peeve. I feel anyone spending hundreds of hard-earned dollars on a bow should

Cam bushing wear can affect cam lean. If you remove the tension from your string and harnesses with a bow press, try to wobble the cam. If it moves easily, you have a worn cam bushing.

get one that works. If you can't tune it, it doesn't work — period. It is like a TV that is fuzzy all the time. You would never buy such a TV, and you would never watch it for several years either. Why buy and use a bow that you can't tune?

Ideally, you will shoot and tune your next bow before you buy it. In fact, I wouldn't buy a bow without first making sure it will tune. If that means you bypass the big box stores and the lure of mail order, so be it. Bows are touchy-feely anyway, and being able to test shoot your next bow is

Before buying a new or used bow, it's best to attempt to tune it. If you can't hit close to your aiming point at 20 yards within a few minor accessory adjustments, you could possibly have a lemon on your hands.

worth any extra expense you incur from buying through a local archery shop.

Yes, you can avoid the problem by trying to tune the bow first. That is fine for the person buying a new bow, but what if you already own a lemon? You can give it to your least favorite cousin or nephew at Christmas and look like a saint, or you can take it back to the place where you bought it and tell them you are not satisfied with a bow that won't tune. I'm not sure how far that will get you, but it is definitely worth a try. Bows you can't tune are miserable. Avoid them at all costs. And considering you're going to make a considerable investment, you should get the best model your money can buy.

LOOKING AHEAD

Now that you've got your hands on a bow that is tunable, the next important part of the equation is your arrow. Tuning arrows is in itself an art form, but learning to do it properly will pay big dividends when heading afield. Follow along in the next chapter as I explain some of the methods for tuning your hunting arrows.

Chapter 30

ARROW TUNING

P erfect accuracy with broadheads requires attention to detail. You work all summer to improve your form and spend several hours getting your bow tuned. Don't allow mediocre performance from your hunting arrows. There's no reason your broadhead groups should be any larger than your field point groups. If they are, your arrows are to blame.

TAKING THE TEST

This will reveal any problems you may have with your hunting arrows. First, number all your arrows so you can identify each one. Attach your broadheads

With a properly tuned bow and practice, there's no reason you shouldn't be as accurate as you are with your field points. Pictured is a group shot at 00 yards with fixed-blade broadheads and field points.

and shoot all the arrows into a target at 20 yards and then 30 yards — stay within your comfort zone. Mark each hole on the target with the corresponding number of the arrow that made it so you can track where all the arrows hit.

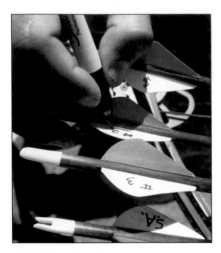

Don't shoot the same arrow over and over. Instead, randomly pick an arrow without looking at the number and shoot your way through the quiver several times. You are likely to see something that will surprise you; a pattern will take shape. The same arrow will hit very nearly the same place each time. Some arrows will fly more accurately from your bow than others. You won't notice this as dramatically when shooting field points (though the differences will still exist). When you attach a broadhead, the differences become magnified.

If you can shoot a fairly tight group with field points, there's no reason you can't shoot an equally tight group with broadheads. The only reason your hunting arrows don't shoot as well as your practice arrows is because the arrows need tuning.

Number your arrows to keep track of individual performance. After shooting each one consecutive times, you'll be able to notice a trend and weed out the flyers. The flyers then can be fine tuned to shoot accurately.

Tuning your bow is important. We've been all through that. But, it is only half of the solution. It will bring your broadhead groups onto the same part of the target as your practice arrows, but bow tuning by itself won't reduce the size of the groups you get when shooting broadheads. To do that, you have to tune each arrow individually. That is what this chapter is all about.

ALIGNMENT IS THE KEY

All the components that make up a hunting arrow must line up perfectly or the effects of wind planing will cause it to fly erratically. One arrow may plane one direction a few inches while the other planes the other way. Pretty soon, you have a much wider group than you expected.

For example, suppose an arrow is slightly bent. Now the broadhead is pointing very slightly off to the side of the intended flight path. When you shoot the arrow, the broadhead will steer it slightly in that direction before the helical fletching kicks in and starts the arrow spinning. Once spinning, the arrow will tend to plane less dramatically. Of course, this is why I don't ever recommend straight fletching. Helical is the only way to go.

The same goes for broadhead alignment. If it isn't installed perfectly straight, it will steer the arrow. Now, if one head is pointing very slightly one direction and the next is pointing very slightly another direction, you end up with some wide groups. The following methods will eliminate this problem and tighten your

Methods For Testing Alignment

Using the two methods listed below, you can test every finished arrow for straightness. If any component is misaligned, it will show up here. The only exception is the arrow's nock; you won't be able to tell if the nock is bent or straight. To be on the safe side, simply replace all your nocks before hunting season.

At one time, I used the V-block (cradle) method of testing my arrows but have since gone to spinning the arrows on my palm because it is faster and no less accurate. However, I have noticed that some people aren't able to make the spin test work. For them, the cradle is much easier to manage.

Spin Test: The spin test is very easy to perform, but does require a little practice. Place the tip of the arrow on a thick spot of skin on the side of your palm and flick the fingers of your other hand to make it spin rapidly. In this way, you will be able to feel every vibration of the arrow no matter how subtle. If you feel any vibration at all where the tip of the broadhead touches your palm, the arrow has misalignment issues. Set it aside for now.

Cradle Test: You may have seen a few "arrow spinners" on the market over the years. They are simply fancy cradles that allow you to hold the arrow in place easily while turning it. You can also substitute a homemade cradle made by cutting notches in opposite sides of an open shoebox. Lay the arrow in the cradle and slowly turn the shaft as you compare the tip of the broadhead to a fixed reference point, such as a dot on a piece of cardboard. The tip should remain still as the arrow shaft turns. If it doesn't, set it aside or attempt to fix the problem.

Spin the finished arrow on your palm to feel if it is perfectly balanced and aligned. If not, you will feel slight vibration. This will verify alignment on everything but the nock.

Alignment is the key to an accurate arrow. Alignment starts with shaft straightness.

broadhead groups considerably.

Shaft Straightness: Your arrows have to be straight or you're sunk before you ever get started. The easiest way to assure straight arrows is to set aside several new arrows you will use only for hunting. Or, if you can't afford to do that, take your shafts to the local archery shop to test them for straightness before you screw on broadheads. You can straighten aluminum arrows, but you can't straighten carbon arrows. If you have a carbon arrow that is dramatically crooked, there is a good chance it is damaged. Stop using it immediately.

However, you can't assume a carbon arrow is perfectly straight if it isn't damaged. Some carbon arrows are made to poor standards. Gener-

Bringing Wayward Arrows Back Into The Group

Nock Tuning: Take the arrows that were not grouping well and work on the nocks. If any show signs of damage from arrow impact, replace them. As mentioned, nocks can also be misaligned when installed. Turn the nocks on all your rogue arrows halfway around to re-seat and hopefully re-align them more perfectly with the shaft.

G5 Outdoors' ASD (Arrow Squaring Device) is the perfect tool to square up arrow ends and inserts for perfect broadhead/arrow alignment.

Go back and shoot these arrows again. Put numbers on each shaft and use a clean target so you can record the numbers next to each hole. After shooting each arrow six more times, you should be able to determine which arrows have improved and which ones will never make it into your hunting quiver.

Broadhead Alignment: The culling isn't finished yet. All your arrows will have to make it past another cut. As I mentioned before, broadhead alignment problems often come down to insert alignment problems. If you have high-quality inserts that press into the shaft and you have done everything to assure alignment but your broadheads still vibrate or wobble when you spin or turn them, there is one more step you can take that often fixes the problem.

If the end of your arrow is not cut off perfectly square to the centerline of the shaft, the broadhead will tend to align with the end of the shaft rather than with the insert. I now use an arrow squaring device (there is currently only one on the market, made by G5 Outdoors) to square up my shafts. This often makes a big difference in how well my arrows spin and is especially important when using arrows that have hidden (fully internal) inserts.

After taking all these steps, you should have several good arrows. If not, I would be shocked and don't really know what other advice to offer.

ally, the top name arrow companies don't offer these. They come from second-tier manufacturers — resellers, actually. The last thing they want you to do is test their straightness. They hope you will just accept the number on their packaging as truth. The only way to make a straight carbon arrow is to throw away all the crooked ones. You can't straighten carbon like you can aluminum, so an unscrupulous manufacturer can try to pass the culls (which would otherwise be discarded or sold for other uses) off as first quality. As I mentioned, you typically won't get that from a reputable arrow maker.

New arrows range from a straightness of +/- .001 to +/- .006 inches. Arrows in this range are fine for most uses. As long as the arrow spins true, it will work great. More about spin testing later.

Again, the very best course is to use new arrows during the hunting season.

Inserts: The insert is the most critical arrow component. If your inserts aren't perfectly centered in the shaft, the broadhead will be pointing to the side. This will cause it to plane offline, which leads to wide groups. Refer to one of the side-

All the components of an arrow are critical, but the insert may be the most critical because it controls the angle of the broadhead. If it is skewed, the broadhead will cause wind planing.

bars accompanying this chapter for methods that you can use to check straightness and alignment. Set aside any arrows that fail this test.

Hopefully, after eliminating the imperfect arrows, you still have enough to hunt with. If not, you'll need to realign or replace your inserts. If you, or the archery shop attendant, installed the insert using hot melt glue, you can realign easily. I use hot melt glue even on my carbon arrows. Many people use epoxy, but to remove the insert or turn the insert you must destroy the arrow. The only exception is when I am installing the small internal inserts that don't shoulder on the end of the arrow. Then I use the supplied epoxy.

You can use hot melt glue with carbon as long as you don't apply the flame directly to the shaft. Instead, apply it to the insert (before installing) or to a field point threaded into the insert when you are trying to remove the insert later.

When the hot melt glue loosens, carefully turn the insert at least one revolution in an effort to float it to the center of the arrow. You may have to do this several times before you have it perfectly aligned, and you may have to remove the insert and add more hot melt glue if it starts to crystallize and become hard to turn after heating.

Fine-tuning inserts isn't as necessary as it was in the early and mid 1990s before manufacturers began to realize that an insert has to be made to tight tolerances and fit snugly into the arrow to assure proper alignment. Today's manufacturers do a much better job, but it is still worth taking this step when alignment is questionable.

You can also replace your inserts with some that fit snugly into the shaft. Forget about using poor quality parts and buy something better. This light press fit is critical to assure proper alignment. If an unglued insert just drops right down in the shaft, it will be difficult to line it up perfectly.

Nocks: Your arrow's nocks must also be straight. Most of the problems related

The easiest way to assure your nocks are straight is to replace them prior to hunting season.

to nocks were eliminated when Easton came out with the Super Nock and Unibushing system. I have seen very few arrows in the past five or six years that still rely on the old-style, glue-on nocks. If you are one of the few still installing tapered nocks, it is time to invest in new arrows. It is as simple as that. If your budget just won't permit a few arrows, make sure your nocks line up when you glue them on by giving them at least one full turn as you push it lightly onto the arrow's taper.

Nocks can also become damaged, and this is not something you will pick up on when testing arrow alignment using the methods I outlined in the sidebar. Nocks take a beating during off-season practice, and to eliminate any concern that your nocks may be bent, simply replace them all. Buy a bag of nocks that are identical to the ones that came with the arrows and swap them out before you start seriously preparing to hunt.

Broadhead Straightness: I have yet to run across a machined, replaceable blade broadhead that wasn't straight, but I have tried several cut-on-contact heads that left a lot to be desired. In fact, back in the late '80s I rigged my first high-performance hunting bow with a one-piece, welded head. While practicing a month before the season I couldn't get the heads to hit the target at 20 yards, let alone the center. Finally, I just gave up and bought some Thunderheads from New Archery Products. Since then, I've learned that some one-piece heads aren't well built. Those models were welded together and the fixtures used to hold the pieces together during the process weren't precise enough to produce perfect alignment suitable for use with a fast bow.

Practice With Your Hunting Arrows

It's finally time to shoot all your best hunting arrows with broadheads installed. Don't worry if the center of your broadhead group is slightly off from the center of your field point group. That's a small point — and if it does bother you, read the next chapter. The important thing is determining whether the arrows group together. If they do, and your bow is well tuned, simply move your sight to bring the group to the center of the target and you're ready for action. One final thing, remember to replace your blades. Even a few shots into foam will dull your sharp broadhead blades sufficiently that they won't cut effectively when shot at game.

Before hunting season starts, be sure to practice with your broadheads to assure your broadhead tipped arrows are grouping together. Also, just prior to the start of the season; replace your blades with new sharp ones or resharpen your heads for a sharper blade.

Much has changed in this regard since the '80s. Now, several of the very well built cut-on-contact heads on the market will perform just fine from a fast compound. So, don't eliminate the entire group. Instead, eliminate the individual heads that aren't up to snuff.

Before you sink your hard-earned cash into a large supply of one-piece heads, buy (or borrow) a couple and try them out using the alignment tests I outlined in one of this chapter's sidebars. You may even want to carry a perfectly straight arrow into your favorite pro shop and go through a few of his heads right there — spinning them in the palm of your hand to see if they are straight. The pro shop

Roll an arrow with a broadhead installed and hold a piece of paper up to act as a fixed reference point. This is a very good way to test for alignment of shaft, insert and broadhead.

owner may not appreciate you exposing sub-par inventory, but then again, poor quality should be exposed. This is the kind of test any pro shop owner should be doing himself before stocking any type of head.

If your broadheads aren't straight, you'll have trouble shooting a tight group. In fact, it will be impossible. Never assume that just because something is on the market it is built perfectly.

Starting with a dozen shafts, by this point you have probably whittled your supply down to six that are perfect. Put your best arrow in the handiest slot in the quiver — that's the one you want to grab first. You will know when you draw it back that it will go exactly where it's aimed — when you see it sizzling through the cold November air homing in on the vitals of a big buck — that, my friends, makes all of this work worthwhile.

LOOKING AHEAD

We have a great shooting bow and hopefully great shooting arrows. Now, it is time to address the question I receive most often. Actually, it is the question I receive second most often. The most often received question is whether or not you need helical fletching. I hope that is clear by now. Next, however, we will conquer the other summit in bowhunting, getting your hunting arrows to hit the same place as your practice arrows.

The micro-tuning I will discuss in the next chapter is for serious archers only. If you are happy moving your sight pins to accommodate your hunting arrow impact point, I have no problem with you. However, if you want to know how you can move that group ever so slightly so you don't have to move your sight pins, this next chapter is for you.

Chapter 31

ADVANCED TUNING WITH BROADHEADS

A s a kid, you no doubt loved to stick your hand out the window of your parent's speeding car just to feel the flow of air. You soon learned that small changes in the direction your fingers were pointing resulted in forces that pulled your hand up, down, right and left. It was great fun and the perfect introduction to aerodynamics. Whether you realized it or not, you learned a valuable lesson about bowhunting too. The wind forces that made your hand shoot up, corkscrew to the left and then slam back down in response to changes in your hand position are the same ones that can make an ill-tuned hunting arrow wind plane out of control.

In the past few chapters, I have gone into detail about bow tuning and arrow tuning; sticking with an earlier analogy, I told you how to make the paper airplane fly straight. The hunting arrow's broadhead must line up with the shaft. The shaft and nock must be straight and the arrow has to leave the bow flying perfectly. If you manage all three of these factors correctly, a hunting arrow will fly just as true as a practice arrow. If any of these pieces are out of whack, the arrow will fly with a mind of its own.

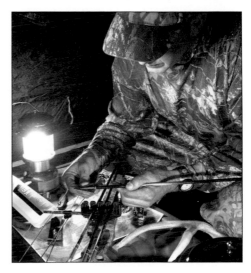

Once they spin true and fly well, broadheads and arrows should be mated for life.

Problems with arrow flight and arrow tuning are the only reasons mechanical broadheads have become so popular in the past half dozen years. While there's nothing wrong with being more accurate in the field (that's one definition of ethical bowhunting), there are still many bowhunters who don't want to switch to mechanical heads for a variety of reasons. If you fall into this category, then this chapter is for you. However, there is also plenty of information here for mechanical broadhead users. While mechanical heads are less sensitive to the problems that plague conventional broadheads, they are not immune. Anything that makes you more accurate with fixed-blade heads will also make you just a small bit more accurate with mechanical heads.

This brings us to the real point of this chapter: tuning. Now we have the ultimate feedback machine — an arrow tipped with a fixed-blade broadhead. This is the true acid test of bow tuning. An arrow may shoot what appears to be a perfect bullet hole through paper and still not be flying straight (very small imperfections in arrow flight are hard to see when paper tuning). When you screw a fixed-blade broadhead on that same arrow and shoot it at 30 yards, you will quickly know if there is still a problem, however.

Getting your broadhead tipped arrows to group with your field point arrows is now easier to achieve. New fixed-blade broadhead designs make tuning easier, especially with today's fast shooting bows.

Every bowhunter has asked the same question at one time or another: "How do I get my hunting arrows to hit the same place as my practice arrows?" I hear it repeatedly, and it would seem to be the greatest mystery in bowhunting. Take heart, it can be done, but you need to complete the following five-step process. Plan to invest a day of your time, possibly a bit more. I have listed the steps here. Some of this is review and where that is the case, I will get straight to the facts.

You can always go back and review past chapters to pick up the needed detail.

THE SYSTEM

Step One: Tuning Your Bow: If the arrow leaves the bow tail high, for example, the broadhead will catch the air, causing the arrow to plane downward and impact low on the target. With a poorly tuned bow, you'll shoot two groups, one with field points and a completely different group with broadheads. Even mechanical broadheads will wind-plane off course if the bow is poorly tuned. To bring the two groups together, your arrows have to leave the bow flying straight.

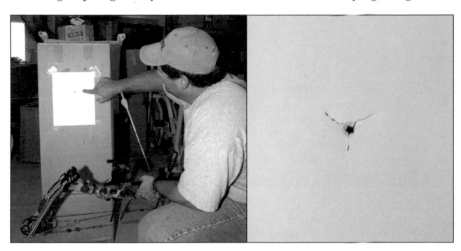

Shooting through paper is the best way to make sure your bow's center shot is accurately set and that your arrows are flying straight. A perfect bullet hole paper tear is the ultimate goal.

I have written a lot about paper tuning in this book, and rather than bog this chapter down with more how-to's, I'm going to suggest you go back and re-read Chapter 21 through Chapter 29. You can also gain additional resources by downloading a copy of Easton's Arrow Tuning and Maintenance Guide. Go to www.eastonarchery.com and click on "downloads" and then on "Tuning Guide." It is enough to understand without any questions that a bow must be tuned perfectly to produce perfect flight with broadheads.

Step Two: Tune Your Arrows: I hammered on this subject in the last chapter. For a hunting arrow to be accurate, all of its components must line up perfectly. I'll summarize quickly.

Nocks: The nock needs to be precisely in line with the shaft. Replace any well-used nocks before you begin a serious tuning session.

Fletching: For stability, you need helical fletching with as much offset as your fletching jig (or the archery shop's fletching jig) can apply.

Typically, long fletching has been the best choice, but today's short, stiff fletching (some with high profile designs) are changing those rules.

Shaft: The arrow shaft must be straight. Keep at least one half dozen shafts that you use just for hunting.

Inserts: Your inserts must be aligned perfectly with the shaft so that your broadheads will line up with the shaft. You may need to square off the end of the arrow if nothing seems to fix a wobbly broadhead.

Step Three: Choosing the Heads: Stick with conservative broadhead designs, those having cutting diameters of one to 1.25 inches. I like the new breed of short heads with stubby blades because they fly well. They have less blade surface so are not as likely to wind plane. Of course, you can also use mechanical broadheads where they are legal because they reduce in-flight surface area even more.

Step Four: Micro-Tuning Your Rest: While the first three steps are review, this step is new and makes up the heart of this chapter. Even if your bow is shooting bullet holes through paper and your arrow components are perfectly aligned, your

Helical fletching with as much offset as you can apply is recommended when shooting broadheads — especially fixed-blade heads.

hunting arrows still may not hit the exact same place as your field points. You have two choices. First, you can live with it and move your sight to bring the broadhead group to the center of your target. Or, you can attempt to fix it and make the broadhead and field point groups the same. The first option requires only an Allen wrench and a couple of hours on the range. The second option requires more tuning, only this time it is what I will refer to as micro-tuning.

I learned micro-tuning from Bob Mizek who works for New Archery Products, a major broadhead manufacturer. These are the steps required to bring your groups together if your bow and arrows are both tuned but your broadheads are hitting slightly off from your field points.

A perfectly aligned arrow is paramount to accuracy when shooting broadhead tipped arrows. Be sure broadhead alignment is flush and check arrow ends after shooting to ensure no damage has occurred.

Broadheads with small blades fly better than those with large blades. Less blade surface equals less resistance.

First, move your rest very slightly in the direction you want your hunting arrows to go. If the broadheads are high or low, left or right of the practice arrows, move the rest very slightly down or up, right or left, respectively. These tweaks are all that's required to point your broadheads along the right initial path to hit the same place as your field points. Expect that you will still have to move your sight pins very slightly after you finish with this step to get both groups back in the center of the target.

Step Five: Advanced Tuning Methods: There are still three aspects of a bow's setup that you can alter in an attempt to fine-tune your bow. First, you can raise and lower your draw weight in small increments. This changes the way the arrow flexes as it leaves the bow and can have a small affect on arrow flight. It is a bigger deal for archers releasing the string with fingers, but will also have an impact, at times, for archers who use a release aid. Typically, a single turn of the Allen wrench will adjust your bow's draw weight by two to four pounds. I would adjust the weight in half turn increments — adjusting both limbs the same amount.

After center shot has been set, small rest adjustments can be made to get your broadheads hitting where your field points hit. Move the rest in the direction you want the broadhead group to move.

You can also affect your arrow flight quickly, easily and sometimes profoundly simply by changing to a different arrow style. That might mean you experiment with stiffer or softer arrows, but even the change from one style to another can have a big affect on arrow flight. I was recently testing bows for an article I was writing. I was getting poor arrow flight from the bows — it seemed they were all junk — so on a whim I decided to change arrows and immediately the arrow flight changed dramatically.

You can adjust tiller by adding or removing turns from one of the limb bolts. Tiller can sometimes produce very slight changes in arrow flight.

If you are struggling to fine-tune your arrow flight and gain that final small improvement in broadhead accuracy, stop by the archery shop and experiment with several different arrows. I think you will be amazed by how much difference this simple change can make.

The third alteration you can make is to your bow's tiller. Remember, this is the measurement from the back of the limb near the limb pocket to a thread tied to both axles. The tiller measurement affects the amount of initial stress on the limbs (how much they are bent before you draw the bow). By altering this systematically, you may be able to change the way the arrow flies. Tiller tuning is a time proven method used by target archers to tighten their long-range groups, but it can also improve your accuracy with fixed-blade broadheads. Again, this adjustment changes the way the arrow flexes as it comes out of the bow.

Start with your tiller measurements the same. Remove a half turn from the top limb bolt to make that limb act softer. Check your nock point location. If it has moved as a result, replace it to the correct location. Now shoot a group to see if the adjustment helped your grouping. If that doesn't help, remove one more half turn from the top limb and again readjust your nock point and test your groupings. Don't adjust the tiller so that one limb is more than one full turn of the limb bolt different from the other.

If this adjustment didn't improve your groupings, restore the bow so it has equal tiller by tightening the top limb to its initial setting. Next, perform the same set of tests by removing weight from the bottom limb by screwing the bottom limb bolt out. Tiller tuning is advanced and requires very good shooting form in order for you to be able to see the subtle differences it makes. It is a fine-tuning technique I would recommend only for experienced archers.

MATES FOR LIFE

Your hunting arrows and broadheads should be lifelong mates. Once you find a broadhead and arrow combination that flies well together, make sure you keep them together for the rest of their natural lives. I even keep my hunting arrows mated from one season to the next.

There are subtle differences in the way various heads seat in various inserts. Sometimes it is as simple as the length of their threads or the flatness of the spacer washer. It can be enough to cause inconsistent accuracy if not addressed. This is why I screw all my broadheads on all my shafts just to find the combinations that spin perfectly. Then I never separate them.

Spin test each arrow to make sure the broadhead is installed in line with the

shaft. In some cases, simply removing the head, flipping the spacer over (if it has one) and screwing it on again will be enough to straighten out small wobbles. Just screwing the head on and off can also affect how it seats and affects its alignment. It's all part of the art and science of hunting arrow accuracy. Regardless of how you arrive at the perfect combination, keep them together. Don't split up a winning team.

ACCURACY WITH MECHANICAL HEADS

Though fixed-blade broadheads are much more sensitive to arrow flight problems than mechanical heads (this is why mechanical heads have gotten to be so popular), that doesn't mean mechanical heads will fly well from a poorly tuned bow. You must still tune your bow perfectly and align all your arrows' components to assure precision accuracy. However, you generally

Spin test each broadhead and arrow combination prior to shooting. If you detect a wobble, try the broadhead on a different arrow and try a different broadhead on the arrow that was wobbling.

eliminate all the fine-tuning I described in steps four and five above. If your bow is shooting a bullet hole and your arrows are tuned, you will shoot most mechanical broadheads very accurately out to normal bowhunting distances.

I would still make every effort to ensure that every arrow spins true and that

Mechanical broadheads are the easiest to get to fly like field points because they have the least exposed blade surface in-flight.

they do, in fact, group with your field points before you take to the field.

Broadhead tuning is a fine art and one that confuses many archers. I hope this chapter has helped remove much of the mystery from this process and set you on the course to shoot your broadheads just as accurately as you shoot your field points.

LOOKING AHEAD

Now you are through with all the heavy work required to ensure proper arrow flight. It is time to move on to the fun stuff — taking the last few steps required to get (and keep) that bow ready for the hunt. Your bow and arrows are tuned; it is time to make the system as hunter friendly as possible. You need a system that doesn't take a lot of thinking or precise execution to shoot well. Well, in fact, it needs to be something that a blithering idiot can shoot effectively because there is some chance that before the season is over, you will be just that. Idiot proofing your bow is a big step; I'll cover that in the next chapter.

Chapter 32

SILENCING AND IDIOT PROOFING YOUR BOW

B y now your bow should be tuned and your sight pins should be set. You should be shooting as well as you've ever shot in your life. Beyond these important steps, there are still a few small things you should do to assure your bow will perform flawlessly when the big moment arrives.

Tighten all the screws and bolts on your bow and use Loctite on the threads to keep them from working loose during the season.

This final gear prep starts with a philosophy. Anything that can go wrong will go wrong. Bowhunters know how true Murphy's Law can be. Take your time and go over your bow with a critical eye. Now is the time to fix every problem, real or imagined, before it costs you a hard-earned opportunity this fall. Be assured, the problems you choose to ignore are the ones that will come back to haunt you.

Sometimes I come through the moment of truth looking good, but all too often, I melt down and turn into a wild-eyed idiot. It is the way the adrenaline rush affects me. But, in spite of this altered state, I'm still expecting to make every shot. With that in mind, here are several things I've done to make my bow as idiot-proof as possible.

The first step to keeping your equipment in tip-top shooting shape is to invest in a quality bow case.

Get a rugged bow case. It is amazing how many bowhunters will go to great lengths to get their bow tuned and sighted in and then just let it bounce around in the back of their pickup all season. Get rid of that flimsy, thin bow case that's little more than a cloth wrap. As a minimum, get one that is heavily padded. Better yet, if you will be hauling the bow over rough roads, get a hard case so you can be certain nothing will be knocked out of kilter. The hunt itself can be hard enough on a bow, there's no reason your bow should take abuse just getting to and from the hunting area.

SOLVE THESE PROBLEMS BEFORE THEY HAPPEN

I'm going to point out all the problem areas. That will surely get you thinking about Murphy's Law and ways to fix things before they go wrong.

Arrow rest moves up or down: Many rests have a separate setscrew to give you two points of contact with the riser. If your rest doesn't have a setscrew, consider drilling and tapping a hole in the mounting frame and installing one. It is an easy project that any hardware clerk can help you prepare.

Arrow falls off the rest: I know of several bucks and bulls that lived longer because an arrow fell off the rest before or during the shot and the archer didn't realize it. This should be a thing of the past with drop-away rests that securely cradle the arrow and rests like the Whisker Biscuit that support it from all sides. If you don't have one of these rests, a simple arrow holder will help in the meantime. You can find them at your local archery dealer or through the major mail order catalogs.

Break a fiber optic pin: Many of today's fiber optic sights still have

Full capture rests keep the arrow from falling off the rest regardless of conditions.

How To Silence Everything

A quiet bow is a tremendous asset in the field. Do everything possible to reduce bow noise. As a minimum, I recommend the following six steps:

1. Install a limb silencer (such as LimbSavers) on your bow limbs to silence the sound of the limbs bottoming.

2. If your bow doesn't have a Teflon cable guard slide, install one. It will quiet your draw noticeably, especially on wet or frosty days. No more game spooking squeaks.

3. Place a layer of Dr. Scholl's moleskin (you can buy it at the pharmacy section of your local grocery store) on your rest to silence the draw.

4. Place a thin layer of adhesive-backed foam or adhesive-backed fleece on the rest shelf to keep rattling arrows from alerting game.

If you plan on hunting with your quiver attached to your bow, be sure and practice with it attached also. Quivers can be a prime source for game spooking noise.

5. Use string silencers.

6. If you will be shooting with your quiver attached, make sure to practice with it on the bow fully loaded with arrows. Quivers can be a source of much noise – some of it can be eliminated with a little common sense and some of it can't. Typically, two-piece quivers are quieter than one-piece models, and if you don't plan to remove the quiver, they are the better choice. Personally, I would rather just remove the quiver when hunting from a treestand to eliminate this source of noise.

amazingly vulnerable filaments that make sweeping, unsupported bends. A twig in the wrong place and they are toast. I used to give a new sight I was testing to our son to play with. If it was worthy of my hunting bow, it came through the 5-year-old boy test in one piece. Few did. There is no easy solution, short of buying a sight with 100-percent fiber support. As a minimum, make sure your top one or two pins are well supported.

Peep sight doesn't rotate: I've never been a big fan of rubber tubing to force a peep sight to rotate. The tubing can break or slip off just when you need it most. If you are patient, you can train your string to deliver the peep sight perfectly every time you draw the bow by first breaking in the string with sev-

Bright sight pins that are well protected will increase your chances for a successful hunt.

Peep sight rotation can ruin a shot if it obscures your vision. Make sure your peep is not rotating or use a peep sight you can see through regardless of rotation.

eral hundred shots and then adding twists and half twists to the bowstring (you will need a bow press) until the peep sight comes back square. Check peep rotation often because it can change if the string gets hot (like in the back seat of a car on a sunny day).

Cable slide squeaks: On wet days, I have had big problems with chattering, squeaking, squealing cable guard slides that actually spooked deer when I drew the bow. It is especially bad with plastic slides on carbon rods after the carbon begins to wear. In all cases, when I switched to a Teflon slide the problems went away.

Nock point slides up: If your nock point is not tight or if your string's center serving separates or slips upward (both are common when a string stretches over time) you may find yourself shooting low — unexpectedly. I have seen some very bad looking center serving on hunting bows that guys are carrying into the field. If you do nothing else, re-serve (or have someone else do it) your bowstring if the serving shows any sign of separating.

String stretches: I mentioned that a string could stretch if it gets too hot, and this is a common problem in warm weather hunts. If you leave the bow in your vehicle when running errands, make sure it is not in direct sunlight and not in a black case. When a string stretches, the nock point moves and the draw length increases; both affect accuracy. I started using custom strings back in 2000 and they were a big step up from those supplied with most bows, but today's bow manufacturers (many of them anyway) are putting better strings on their bows. Custom strings are still a good idea; they just aren't mandatory on every bow like they were just a couple of years ago.

Arrows: A friend of mine recently missed a nice 150-inch plus 10-pointer

Check your nocks every day and make sure they are free of debris. A dirty nock can lead to many problems that affect accuracy and getting the shot off.

because his nocks were filled with mud and he never noticed it when he snapped the first arrow on the string. The nock held but it was not fully engaged. When Larry drew the bow, the arrow came off, bounced on the stand and dropped to the ground. Larry grunted to try to hold the buck while he scrambled for another arrow. Unfortunately, it too had a nock-full of mud. By the time Larry got the nock cleaned out and on the string, he was too rattled to make a good shot.

Adjust your quiver so the ends of your arrows are inside the bottom cam. That way, when you set the bow on the bottom cam, or when you pull it up into your tree stand, there is less chance the nocks will fill with dirt. Of course, it also pays to take a close look at everything once you get on stand.

Vibration loosens screws: Lightweight arrows produce lots of vibration that the bow must soak up after the arrow is gone. This has the tendency to loosen screws

If your arrows extend beyond the bottom cam of your bow, you risk filling the nocks with dirt, possibly hurting your chances for a quick shot.

and nuts. Once you know you are tuned and sighted in, it's time to lock everything down so there is no way a screw or nut can vibrate loose and create trouble halfway through the season. A drop of semi-permanent blue Loctite (www.henkel.com) on all the threads will hold everything together through a tough season.

Hiding the bow: Several years ago, I was hunting in Newfoundland when I set off on a long stalk. The guide remained behind on a high rock to give hand signals. I was gone for the better part of the day because my stalk covered many miles. Later the guide told me that at times I was so far away that all he could see of me through the binoculars was the shine of sunlight off my bow limbs. Say what?

Since then I've made it a point to put cloth camouflage tape on any solid limb bows that can have the potential to pro-

If you have to shoot quickly, it helps if you don't have a wrist sling on your bow.

duce glare. Cloth tape is better than paper tape because it is rougher and doesn't shine.

A FAST HANDLING BOW

Sometimes you need to shoot fast. An idiot-proof bow will accommodate this need with no interference. In other words, get rid of any pre-shot rituals that only take time without making you more accurate. Remember, the best pre-shot routine is the one with the least number of steps. And the best bow setup is one that eliminates all the roadblocks to full draw.

Grip area: I've had a few quick shots in the past couple of years in which I struggled to quickly get my hand through the wrist sling. In each case, it was distracting. Now, I do all my shooting without a sling to speed up the process and remove one more step from the pre-shot routine. Today's bows have narrow grips and thin handles that make shooting without a sling very practical. You can wrap your fingers lightly around the grip section to maintain total control of the bow without choking the handle.

Nocking point: Don't take the decision of whether to use a string nocking loop too lightly. I still prefer to attach my caliper release directly to the string; even though loops have certain advantages. It's debatable, but I feel I can hook up more reliably going straight to the string. I use a standard rubber donut under the nock and dress the center serving with a layer of Fast Flight string strand material to reduce wear on the serving caused by the release jaws. I inspect the serving and change the over-wrap often. This has worked for years without a single hiccup.

I have experimented with a loop for hunting and felt uneasy about it the entire time. I never felt 100 percent positive I could snag the loop after my adrenal gland emptied itself into my blood stream. However, I will say that I had five shots at

Being able to shoot quickly is an advantage. Loop hook releases load easily to a string loop and offer a crisp, smooth release.

Shooting a practice arrow from your treestand instills confidence in your shooting and assures your setup is still accurate.

deer and never had any problems. This decision comes down to personal preference, but if you go with the loop, at least choose a release aid that hooks up easily and quickly.

THE BEST STEPS YOU CAN TAKE

I have a friend who religiously carries a practice arrow with him in his quiver. When Dan arrives at his stand for an afternoon hunt, the first thing he does is take a practice shot in the direction he will be walking when he climbs down to leave. He does the same thing after full light in the morning when the woods settle down. This simple step assures his bow is hitting where he is aiming.

If something suspicious happens during one of these practice shots, or if he badly misses the leaf he is aiming at, he knows it is time to study the bow to see if something has moved and then get the target out when he gets back to camp to find out what went wrong.

Go through everything on your bow every time you settle in the stand. While it may be too late to fix a problem, at least you will have time to figure out a workaround strategy that allows you to make accurate shots despite the problem. Though it is never fun to uncover a problem, it is always better to do it before you miss the big one.

MAKING YOUR BOW QUIET

I have tagged several deer over the years after missing them with the first shot. In some cases, a doe jumped the string (dropped down at the shot) and I shot over her, but in other cases, I simply missed. I remember one buck in particular. I don't think he even heard the first shot. A quiet bow is a more effective bow. There is

To make your bow as quiet as possible install limb dampeners and string silencers. This not only helps quiet the bow but also soaks up vibration.

no doubt in my mind that a quiet bow will improve your success rate, because it reduces the affects of string jumping and increases the odds of getting a second shot.

Start with a design that is fairly quiet right out of the box. Before you buy your next bow, test shoot a number of them to make sure the one you buy is very quiet. Next, add limb silencers. From there, you can make further incremental improvements by using other noise reducing products and by looking for a sight and rest that don't vibrate when you twang the string.

Having an idiot-proof bow is not to imply that you are some kind of idiot. In fact, you have to be pretty wise to head off all the problems that can arise while bowhunting. If, in your wildest dreams, you can imagine something going wrong, then it is worth fixing before it happens for real. If I could add one thing to Murphy's Law it would be this: If it can go wrong it will go wrong — and probably when you are shooting at the biggest bucks of your life. If Murphy had been an bowhunter, that is what he would have said. Don't wait until it happens before you fix it.

Use adhesive-backed fleece to silence your sight window and areas of your riser that are prone to arrow contact.

LOOKING AHEAD

There is one piece of equipment I haven't discussed in this book and that is the quiver. There are trade-offs you must make when deciding which style to use and how to keep it quiet when you shoot. In the next chapter, I will go over these important decisions.

Chapter 33

QUIVER TRADE-OFFS

I n an ideal world, you wouldn't shoot your bow with a half dozen arrows hanging off the side. But when it comes to practical considerations in the real world, the bow quiver is certainly an excellent option. When you head off on a long stalk through thick cover or tote your bow to your treestand in the dark of predawn, the last thing you want is a half dozen arrows flopping all over the place.

There are certainly tradeoffs. For example, adding weight and surface area to your bow can only degrade accuracy, but the options are worse. I have done enough testing myself and interviewed very effective archers that use a bow quiver anyway. Here is why.

THE ISSUE OF ACCURACY

I've heard well-respected hunters with opinions that ran all over the map when it comes to quivers. Some use bow quivers and feel they make no difference at all while others would not be caught dead with a quiver on their bow.

Rather than rely on guesswork and emotional arguments, I called Randy Ulmer. Randy didn't disappoint me. As I expected, he has actually tested bows with and without a quiver attached to see how much difference it makes.

A bow quiver is the best way to transport hunting arrows to the treestand.

First, he selected a group of very accomplished archers and came up with the control group. Each archer shot five arrows at 40 yards with bow-mounted quivers full of arrows. Then they removed one arrow at a time while shooting five

arrows at each juncture until their eight-arrow quivers were empty. They didn't do anything to compensate for the quiver; they simply held their sights dead on.

Randy and his group of ringers ended up with 36 five-arrow groups, which they carefully measured at each stage in the test. All this meticulous testing yielded a conclusion; they found that the point of impact moved less than two inches at 40 yards when comparing a full quiver to an empty one.

This amount of accuracy lost is totally insignificant for two reasons. First, if you have the quiver and arrows on the bow when practicing and sighting in, you will notice no difference in accuracy when you remove just one arrow and put it on the string. Second, even if you practice all summer without a bow quiver and don't ever change your sights to compensate, you will experience only a small change in impact at normal bowhunting ranges when you add a full quiver to the bow. Besides, how many

Shooting with a quiver on your bow does add weight and more surface area but doesn't have to dramatically affect accuracy. Practice diligently with your quiver attached prior to the start of the season.

bowhunters carry eight arrows these days? Most carry four arrows. With fewer arrows, the change in your bow's balance will be less and the amount your impact point changes will also be less — insignificant for all practical purposes.

Now for my exception! I don't like shooting a bow in the wind when I am using a bow quiver. The arrows increase the bow's surface area and make it harder to hold the bow steady. If you want to eliminate this possible negative affect you can simply use a detachable quiver and take it off when a shot is imminent. If the quiver isn't detachable, you can remove the arrows and lay them beside you on the ground. This precaution may stabilize your sight pin slightly while aiming.

Many bowhunters who hunt from treestands use detachable bow quivers

When using a detachable quiver, be conscious of where you put it. If the chance for a second shot presents itself, you need to be able to grab an arrow quickly.

to transport their bows to and from the stand. While hunting, they take the quiver off and hang it in the tree within easy reach. This is my approach.

THE ISSUE OF MOBILITY

There is no doubt having a quiver on your bow will affect accuracy. Randy's testing made that clear. However, there are still few better places to carry your arrows. With a bow quiver, you have the arrows right at your fingertips where you can keep track of them. You won't suddenly look down to find you have lost a couple somewhere behind you in the brush. Also, because the top limb and the quiver hood acts as deflectors, of sorts, you can slide your bow and arrows through some of the thickest brush imaginable with no fear that you'll snag an arrow.

The most common alternatives include a hip quiver and a back quiver. Hip quivers tend to be noisy as you slip through the

Many treestand hunters use detachable quivers when hunting, and once they get to their treestand, they remove it and hang it close to them in easy reach.

brush. The arrows catch when you walk and their fletchings make noise as they slide across sticks and branches — especially if you use feathers. A hip quiver

A bow quiver can be the best option when stalking and crawling. The quiver hood acts as a shield and protects the arrows from being knocked out.

Bow-mounted quivers need to have solid arrow grippers. When stalking on the ground or through thick brush, you can't afford to be dropping arrows.

points 180 degrees in the wrong direction for crawling. The arrow nocks point forward and the hood trails behind — a design that's ideal for one thing only: snagging arrows in the brush.

Back quivers are more manageable than hip quivers, and will serve as a fine way to get arrows to a treestand, but they also have shortcomings when you are stalking. This is probably a bit more of a personal decision than one based on hard logic, but when I'm crawling through brush I want everything right in front of me where I can see it. I don't want anything on my back that can grab brush and increase the size of my profile making me more visible. I may have to crawl through a tight spot or roll over onto my back to get around an obstacle. It's easier to do both when the quiver is on my bow.

There is no situation where a bow quiver is going to get you in trouble. The same cannot be said about the other systems you can use. That's why I favor the bow quiver — it doesn't slow me down and it doesn't limit what I can do in the field.

Today's quivers feature noise dampening components to battle vibration and noise. Fuse Accessories incorporates shock rods into their hoods. This affords a smoother and quieter shot.

Two-piece quivers are durable and great for stalking. However, you typically don't have the ability to detach them.

CHOOSING THE RIGHT BOW QUIVER

Not all bow quivers are created equal. A poorly chosen bow quiver has almost as much negative affect on your ability to hunt easily as a hip or back quiver. First, the perfect bow quiver must have tight arrow grippers. If you shoot carbon arrows (and nearly everyone does these days), you need a quiver that will hold them tightly. The only frustrations I have had with bow quivers occurred when the arrows fell out. That is frustrating. Sometimes, the arrow grippers lose their hold when they get cold, but if you have to err, choose a quiver that is very tight.

Second, a good bow quiver should not be noisy. Noise comes from loose parts that vibrate during the shot. The previous generation of quiver designs often made a bow noisier because the quiver hood amplified bow vibration. However, many of today's more rugged designs actually make a bow quieter because they are flexible and soak up vibration with a hood design that doesn't amplify noise.

Third, the quiver should be adjustable up and down so you can use it on a short bow without the arrow nocks extending beyond the bottom cam where they can fill with dirt. This is a very important consideration when shooting a short bow.

DETACHABLE VS. TWO-PIECE

I use a detachable quiver when hunting from a treestand and a two-piece quiver when stalking game and hunting on the ground. The two-piece quiver is more solid, in most cases, so it holds up better to the rigors of rough country foot hunting. And, of course, the detachable quiver works great in places where you will be waiting in ambush.

The bow-mounted quiver is the best suited quiver for most bowhunters.

CONCLUSION

You have three basic styles of quivers from which to choose. First, you have hip quivers, which I feel are a poor choice for all but target shooting situations. Second, you have back quivers, which are more easily navigated through thick cover than hip quivers but still are prone to hang up on brush. Finally, you have bow-mounted quivers that offer the best overall performance for most bowhunters. They permit you to control your arrows better than the other two styles and when the situation permits, you can remove the quiver for the shot.

LOOKING AHEAD

All the pieces of your bowhunting rig are in place and they are all working great. The next chapter is dedicated to helping you keep them that way. Maintenance may not be very glamorous, but it is essential. Think of it as one of the small details that add up to produce a successful season. It is easier to get fired up about maintenance when you can see the direct correlation between a few hours of effort and more filled tags.

Chapter 34

MAINTAINING YOUR BOW

J ust as your auto mechanic will tell you that regular maintenance is much less expensive than major overhauls, the same applies to your bow. Pay me now or pay me later. Obviously, keeping your bow shooting well this season is a high priority. Here are the things you should watch for and methods for keeping the bowhunting bogeyman from ruining your season.

ROUTINE ITEMS

You should wax your strings and harnesses anytime they show signs of drying out. When they dry out, they will appear frayed and fuzzy. A quick application of the proper wax will seal the string, prevent fiber-to-fiber abrasion and keep the string and harnesses from absorbing moisture. Waxing the string will prolong

String maintenance is priority number one when owning a bow. Treat your string like it's the most important part of the bow.

its life. The Dacron strings used more than a decade ago required true wax to keep them in proper repair, but today's modern synthetics (Dyneema, Spectra and Vectran) do best with specially formulated lubricants that are part oil and part wax. I care for my string and harnesses every two weeks during the fall.

You can also prolong your harness life by smoothing out the slots in your cable guard slide. These can have sharp edges that the harnesses rub against, but a few minutes with a small rattail file will fix that.

Wax your string and cables often to prolong the life of your string. When purchasing a bow, always buy a stick of wax.

Install new moleskin on your rest launchers regularly so they remain quiet during the draw. I change mine several times each season to make sure they aren't wearing thin. Some carbon arrows are abrasive and they will eat through your moleskin much faster than aluminum arrows will.

I also replace the over-wrap on my center serving regularly. I attach my caliper release directly to the bowstring, and in the area of contact I apply a double layer of Fast Flight fiber from a dead string. I replace this layer shortly before the season each year to assure it is tight. This is also a good time to inspect the serving underneath for separation and damage.

STRING AND HARNESS STRETCH

All synthetic systems stretch with use, up to a point. This is especially true under adverse conditions (heat and moisture). I once shot a 3-D tournament with a past editor of Petersen's Bowhunting magazine on a hot, rainy day. He went from shooting dead-on to shooting a foot low at 30 yards simply because his string stretched and his nock point moved up. This was back in the days when basic Fast Flight was the only option. While today's systems are much more resistant to stretch, they are still vulnerable.

With single-cam and hybrid-cam bows, minor harness stretch is much less detrimental to arrow flight. That is the good news. However, string stretch, when it occurs, is still a problem. It causes your nock point to move and your draw weight and draw length to increase.

I check string stretch two ways. First, I keep a T-square handy and continually check my nock point to make sure it hasn't moved. However, regular shooting will also reveal stretch, as your arrow groups will mysteriously move slightly down for a two-cam system or up for a single-cam system. The second way you can detect string stretch is to keep a close watch on your cam rotation. Many bows now offer tuning marks on the cams to assure that they stay within the factory default settings for optimum arrow flight and performance. At the very least, take a few measurements from the string to the lobes on your cam or cams and make sure that distance doesn't change over time.

Take measurements prior to tuning in a new bow and check those measurements throughout the life of that bow. By using a T-square, you'll be able to see if your nocking point has changed and your string has stretched.

STRING SERVING

I've already spent a lot of space in this book discussing string serving. I won't belabor the point here, but I will restate it. Make sure your serving has not separated and is not showing signs of wear where the loop attaches or where your release hooks to the string (if you connect directly to the string). I have a simple rule: never trust factory serving unless the bow is equipped with a high-quality custom string.

CAM TIMING

If you shoot a traditional two-cam bow, you should check your cam timing every few days. Draw the bow and compare the position of the cams as they roll over. They should both reach their full draw position at the same time. In other words, the harnesses should touch the ends of their tracks together. If they don't, the bow will not shoot well.

If the timing is off, relax the tension on the string and harnesses and add a twist to the harness attached to the cam that is reaching full draw first. Draw the bow a few times to assure everything is settled in place and then test the timing again. Repeat until you get it perfect. You may even need to go in half-twist increments to really nail it.

During hunting season, check your equipment at least once a week to make sure everything is tight and secure.

KEEP EVERYTHING TIGHT

If you are hunting every day, go over your bow at least once per week to make sure all your nuts and screws are still tight. I once missed a very nice Pope and Young class eight-pointer in Illinois because my rest came loose and moved. I shot right under his brisket at just 15 yards. I will never let that happen again. Now I check everything regularly.

LIMB PROBLEMS

Limb failure still sometimes occurs even with modern compound bows. The most frequent limb problem is lifting or splintering along the tension side (front) of the limb. You will see (or feel) sharp, jagged pieces of fiberglass sticking out from the limb edges. Generally, this is not a big problem. You can simply clip them off close to the limb with a wire cutter. However, if the separation or lifting continues and becomes worse, the limb can fail in this area. Keep a close eye on it.

A second type of limb failure is cross-sectional cracking of the limb tip. This crack will appear on the limb's end parallel to the axle. This mode of cracking generally results from dry firing the bow or shooting super light arrows repeatedly. You may first notice erratic arrow flight before actually becoming aware of the crack itself. Obviously, you should not shoot a bow in this condition. Take it to your dealer immediately.

Check your limbs regularly for cracks. The stress side of the limb is typically where splinters and cracks are found.

The third type of limb failure is less damaging but should still be fixed immediately. A crack may start in the bottom of the limb forks with a solid limb bow and grow down the center of the limb. This damage can occur if you nick your limb fork on a hunt. Because of the stresses that affect this area of the limb, the nick can quickly grow into a crack.

CAM BUSHINGS

Some bows have bearings between the axles and the cams, but many still use bushings. Only a few years ago, all the cams used bushings. If your bow has bushings instead of bearings, you should check them at least once every year. Now would be a good time, when you are thinking about it. If you shoot your bow a lot during the off-season, you will eventually wear out your cam bushings. This will affect your arrow flight and your accuracy.

The easiest way to check your cam bushings is to put your bow in a bow press and relieve the tension on the string and harnesses so that there is no force on the cams. Try to wobble the cams back and forth. If they move easily, the bushing is wearing out. I would wait until the cam wobbles more than one eighth-inch total before making the upgrade.

SHOOT REGULARLY

The best way to keep your bow in good working order during the season is to shoot it regularly so you can head off any problems before they cost you a trophy. Ideally, you should shoot every day, but even every other day will help not only to keep the bow in shape, but will also keep your shooting muscles in shape.

The best way to check your cam bushings is to put your bow in a bowpress and take tension off the string. Wiggle the cams and if they move more than ⅛-inch, it's probably time to replace your cam bushings.

Shoot all year long to develop good shooting habits and to keep your bow in tune. Ideally, you should try to fling a few arrows every day.

STORING YOUR BOW

Today's bows are very stable and durable. They are not subject to changes during storage. Older style bows (especially the laminated limbs found on bows made 10 years ago) had a shelf life. Today's bows really don't change as long as you take a few basic precautions. Store your bow in your home, not in your garage where it will be subject to extremes in temperature — and definitely not in your car or truck. It is wise to back the poundage off a couple of turns on each limb bolt, but that is not critical. That's it.

You should be able to put your bow away in January and pick it up in July and expect it to hit the same place it did when you put it away. Your string may stretch a little, but that is the only thing that is likely to change.

LOOKING AHEAD

Now it is time to put all this newfound technical savvy to good use. In the next chapter I will discuss the final steps you can take to ensure accuracy while hunting, including a few gear tweaks and practice tips. You are almost ready. Just one more stop on the journey.

Chapter 35

FINAL PREPARATION

T hough you can't control luck, you can control several of the ingredients that allow you to take full advantage of luck when it comes stumbling down the trail. I've had my share of good luck through the years, and I would be the first to admit that plenty of things beyond my control have fallen into place in order to get those short-range shots. But I don't feel making the shots themselves was based on luck. I would hate to enter a season hoping I could make the necessary shots. I want to do everything possible to be sure I am ready for the challenges I will face. Hoping for a good hit is setting yourself up for failure.

We are getting toward the end of our journey, and it is now time to screw on your broadheads for real; you need to know you can make the shots that you are likely to face.

The final few weeks before you start hunting is the perfect time to fine-tune and tweak the details so your confidence and skills both peak at just the right time. Now is not the time to knock the dust off your bow and perform major surgery on your shooting form. It's

During the weeks preceding the bowhunting opener, practice as much as possible. This is the perfect time to fine tune your form so you'll be shooting as well as you can.

too late for that. Now is the time to get all the details in perfect order. Here are five elements of preparation that you should focus on during those important final two weeks.

FINAL EQUIPMENT CHECK

As I have stated several times in this book, one of the most likely problem areas in any bow is the string and harness system. The fibers can easily become damaged and worn during the off season. They also may have stretched during hot summer days spent sitting in your car or truck. A stretched string will increase your draw length and change your nock point location.

Replace your sight pins with some that are highly visible during all legal shooting hours.

Start shooting your broadheads at least a month before the bowhunting season opens. This will give you plenty of time to fine tune your setup.

If your string is only stretched, you can reset it easily by simply removing one end and twisting it in the direction of the existing spiral until the bow once again makes the proper draw length. If the string or harness is damaged, however, you'll need to replace them. With a two-cam bow, you should never replace just one harness because it will stretch at a different rate from the one that is already broken in and will continually cause your bow to go out of time.

Now is also last call for any sight pin changes. While it is too late to break in a whole new method of shooting, it is not too late to replace your top pin with one of a different color (I prefer green for the top pin because it appears brighter to me) or replace it with one of a different design.

For the most part, bows are nearly indestructible. I have traveled a lot during the last 15 years while hunting and the only time I needed to use my backup bow (which I always take with me on trips) was when a guy backed over my number one bow with his Suburban. And then it was only a precaution. When I got home and had time to check things over very carefully, the primary bow was just fine.

If a bow is going to go bad, it is generally in one of two places. The first is the string and harness system, as I have already explained. You will also pull your hair out when a screw comes loose and your rest or sight changes position. I mentioned it in Chapter 32, but it bears repeating here. Consider removing all the mounting hardware on your bow and adding a drop of Loctite 242 (the blue stuff) to the threads so they won't accidentally back out or rattle loose during the course of the season.

HUNTING ARROW READINESS

After making any equipment changes, getting your arrows ready to hunt should be the next priority. There is no better way to tell if you are ready than to screw on the broadheads and start practicing. Spend at least 25 percent of your practice time during the last two weeks with broadheads on your bow. It can be challenging to find a good broadhead target, but you can't go wrong simply using a basic, inexpensive closed cell foam target. You can find them at most archery shops.

By practicing with your broadheads, you will gain confidence and head off any problems before they occur in the field. While you are at it, make sure to practice regularly from an elevated position to simulate shooting from a treestand (if you will be hunting from a treestand).

With at least three weeks remaining before the season, you have plenty of time to work out any problems with tuning and component alignment and still have time left over to work on the shots you'll need while hunting.

SHOTS TO PRACTICE

While it may feel good to stand at 20 yards on the range using perfect form and shooting tight groups, true preparation isn't about feeling good. True preparation is about honestly trying to find your weaknesses while you still have time to fix them.

I can't remember a shot at real game in which I was able to use classic shooting range form. Most often, I find myself sitting, twisting, leaning, kneeling — in general doing everything but standing up straight. Because game rarely does what we expect, we need to be ready for every kind of awkward shot imaginable. Good shooting form will carry you through many of these situations, but preseason practice under tough conditions will produce confidence and allow you to find your tendencies when things aren't perfect.

Practice awkward shots just as regularly as you practice using perfect form.

Use maximum concentration with every shot you take. Take every shot with the deliberation you would take if it were going toward the biggest buck of your life.

For example, I tend to shoot to the left when I have to turn to my right. Knowing this, I always try to position my stands, or my body, to reduce the chances of such a shot, but when it is presented, I've learned that I have to keep my upper body cranked hard to the right until the arrow hits or I will pull it left. Some bowhunters tend to shoot low when they are kneeling or sitting flat on the ground. You need to learn these kinds of things when shooting at a target, not at a big buck.

Do all of this practice while you are wearing your standard hunting clothing. You will learn which shot angles create problems with bulky clothing and which ones require an arm guard. You will also find that shooting with a facemask and gloves creates a completely different feel. This type of practice doesn't need to take more than a few sessions, but it is very important preparation.

QUALITY OVER QUANTITY

You can sum up hunting accuracy in one simple sentence: Pick a spot you want to hit and focus on it with all your might until the arrow hits. During the last week or two before you plan to start hunting, increase your concentration while practicing. Don't let your mind wander. Become accustomed to shooting with maximum mental effort focused on the spot you are trying to hit. Don't shoot as many arrows as you normally would, but shoot each one as well as you possibly can. Now every shot should be treated like it's the most important one of your life, because in a few weeks it may be for real.

This kind of focused practice paid huge dividends for a friend of mine when he shot a giant buck a couple of seasons back. It was a deer that Larry was hunting and had been seeing on and off for several months. It was a monster that later

Practice in realistic hunting conditions because quality is more important than quantity

held the state record for a short time. Under such conditions, it would be very easy to choke when the buck actually showed up, but Larry kept his cool and made a great shot.

He credited his ability to stay calm to the fact that during his pre-season practice sessions, he had imagined he was aiming each practice arrow at the big buck. He even went so far as to visualize the buck standing there, massive rack and all. After a couple of weeks of this kind of practice, Larry was more than ready when the time came to make good on his daydream.

Getting ready for the season is often just as much fun as actually hunting. Excitement runs high and optimism is boundless. This will be the year you mix it up with Old Mossyhorns. But unless you take the time to cover the details during the last two weeks of preparation, it may be the year when Old Mossy gives you the slip. Take the time to prepare properly and you will be able to relax with the confidence that comes from true preparation. You won't have to hope you can make the shot; you will know you can.

LOOKING AHEAD

It's time to wrap this up and go hunting. I am sure that by now you are shooting the best you have ever shot and are holding a bow that is producing excellent arrow flight and amazing accuracy. Enjoy the season — it should be a good one.

Chapter 36

SUMMARIZING THE KEY POINTS

I n this last chapter, I am going to condense the key points of this book so that when you put it down, you will remember the most important information.

BOWS ARE SIMPLE MACHINES

If you reduce all the mechanics of your bow to two principles, they would be leverage and energy storage in a spring. The cams utilize leverage to make the bow flex and store energy in a pair of stiff springs (the limbs) while at the same time making the string easier to hold back at full draw (letoff). The angle of the limbs and the way the cams apply leverage (their shape) are the main elements making up a bow.

THE GRIP IS IMPORTANT

How the bow feels in your hand makes a difference in how well you will be able to relax while shooting the bow. Relaxation translates into

You will realize a compound bow is a simple machine once you see that it is nothing more than a system of levers.

How you grip the bow affects your shooting consistency and accuracy.

accurate shooting. Most bowhunters find that a narrow grip allows them to shoot more accurately, because the point of contact between their hand and the bow is smaller, producing less ability to apply torque to the bow.

IMPROVING YOUR VISIBILITY

You can improve your visibility of the target and your pins in low light while shooting more accurately at the same time if you switch to a large, quarter-inch diameter peep sight and a spooled fiber optic sight with a round pin guard. By centering the entire pin guard inside your peep sight, you maintain precision while at the same time enjoying the improved light transmission offered by the large peep.

BOW TUNING IS NOT COMPLICATED

You can break bow tuning up into the simple elements and the advanced elements. Generally, you can tune a modern bow using only the simple elements. They are nock point position (move it up or down) and rest position (move it

Choosing a sight with a round pin guard and then coupling it with a large peep will improve visibility without sacrificing accuracy.

up, down, left or right). That's not too much to absorb, really.

If your bow won't tune properly using simple techniques, it is time to move on to the advanced techniques. These include cam timing (may be an issue for single- or hybrid-cam bows but often an issue for two-cam bows). Also consider arrow stiffness and fletching style. You can experiment easily with various shafts and fletching at the archery shop. A drop-away or full-capture arrow rest is another advanced element that can quickly fix poor arrow flight resulting from fletching contact. Other advanced techniques include increasing or decreasing your draw weight and changing your bow's tiller setting.

UNTUNABLE BOWS

Rarely will you be required to get very far into the advanced elements before your bow is shooting great. However, there is one dark secret some bow manufacturers would rather you never uncover: not every bow is tunable. I have come across many bows (less in recent years) that could not be tuned. In all cases, this was the result of improper, erratic nock travel. The manufacturers didn't design the bow well enough to produce a nock that goes straight back and straight forward without deviating up, down or to either side. The only way to know if you own or are about to buy a lemon is to attempt to tune the bow. If you can't tune it, get rid of it or don't buy it.

ARROW TUNING MAKES A HUGE DIFFERENCE

There are two levels of tuning that contribute to good hunting accuracy. Bow tuning will bring your hunting arrow groups onto the same part of the target as your practice arrow groups. That is one level. The second level is arrow tuning. By tuning each arrow individually, you can decrease the size of your hunting arrow groups. You need to do both.

Fortunately, arrow tuning is simple. Make sure all the components making up the arrow are perfectly lined up with a straight shaft and you have an accurate hunting arrow. There are simple tests you can perform to determine if your arrows fit this description, such as spinning them on your palm to sense vibration or rolling them in a notched fixture to see if the tip of the broadhead moves.

PRACTICE THE WAY YOU HUNT

Don't fall for the temptation to only practice your strengths. That won't make you a better bowhunter. Instead, look for awkward situations to test and improve your skills. In other words, it is

Arrow tuning is just as critical as bow tuning. Not all arrows fly straight out of the box. A few simple adjustments can be made to get you hitting bull's-eyes.

tempting to simply stand in the yard making perfect shots using perfect form, but that isn't the way you will actually hunt. Look for realistic conditions and learn how you must adjust your form to compensate for these tougher shooting conditions. Be sure to include several practice sessions spent wearing

The best way to practice is as if you were hunting. Before the season starts and during the season as the temperatures change, practice with your hunting clothes on.

your hunting clothes from elevated shooting positions (if you will hunt from a treestand) so you can get used to the feel of your bulky jacket, gloves and face-mask in a real hunting situation.

You should plan to do most of your pre-season practice with broadheads attached to your arrows. While it is sure nice to have your broadhead-tipped hunting arrows group in exactly the same place as your field-point tipped practice arrows, that is not critical. You can easily move your sight body to bring the broadhead group onto your intended impact point. You can try to fine-tune your broadheads so they hit the same hole as your field points. However, if you hit a wall, don't get discouraged. It is common to have to move your sight body slightly to bring it all together.

Bow tuning is not as hard as most people think. The ability to successfully tune, tweak, and keep your bow shooting accurately, makes you a better bowhunter.

CONCLUSION

Sure, there is a lot more in this book when we get into the details of how you actually do all these things, but if you keep these simple steps in mind, you will be well on your way to shooting better than you have ever shot in your life. I've enjoyed the opportunity to bring you this information and hope it makes your hunting more enjoyable and more successful.